9.75

MORE ESSAYS ON RELIGION

MORE ESSAYS ON RELIGION

BY

ARTHUR CLUTTON-BROCK

WITH AN INTRODUCTION BY
CANON B. H. STREETER

Essay Index Reprint Series

BOOKS FOR LIBRARIES PRESS
FREEPORT, NEW YORK

First Published 1928
Reprinted 1971

INTERNATIONAL STANDARD BOOK NUMBER:
0-8369-2349-9

LIBRARY OF CONGRESS CATALOG CARD NUMBER:
76-156632

PRINTED IN THE UNITED STATES OF AMERICA

PREFACE

A RTHUR CLUTTON-BROCK gave little serious attention to religion until rather late in life; and he then approached it from the point of view of a mind formed by a life-long enthusiasm for literature and art. His earlier attitude was almost light-heartedly full of hope. But towards the end of his life, without losing his hope, he began to give deeper thought to the difficulties in the way of any solution of the mystery of the Universe. The volume *Essays in Religion*, published posthumously in 1925, represented this latest phase. It was made up almost entirely of unprinted material, being in fact the first draft of chapters of what he intended to be a connected and carefully considered treatise. The present volume consists in the main of reprinted pieces, and it represents the earlier phase; but that means that it represents the man as he was known to most of his friends before disease had begun to undermine his almost boyish exuberance of spirit.

B. H. S.

The Queen's College
Oxford
July, 1927

V

CONTENTS

MORE ESSAYS ON RELIGION

I

Crashaw's Christmas Poems ◦ ◦

IF anyone tried to choose a Christmas
anthology out of the English poets he
would find it difficult to fill even a small
book with good verses. Most poems about
Christmas have more piety than poetry in
them ; yet the Nativity of Christ seems a
subject made for poetry, and, in particular, is
well suited to the German side of our imagination, with its mixture of mystery and homeliness, its contrast of the manger and the
visiting Kings of the East, of the shepherds
lying among their flocks in the snow and the
midnight heavens opening above them to
reveal a choir of angels singing tidings of great
joy. The theme has been worthily treated in
German music, and in earlier Italian art, but
hardly in English poetry ; for those of our
poets whose genius would seem best fitted to
treat it have strangely neglected it. Blake,

for instance, the master of homely mystery,—
what a poem might he have written on the
Nativity! Yet he has not left us a single
carol. There is, indeed, one by a nameless
author of the fifteenth century that Blake
might have written :

> He came all so still
>   Where His Mother was,
> As dew in April
>   That falleth on the grass.

But hardly anything has been written since in
this beautiful manner, and nothing by Blake.
Indeed, when the Nativity has stirred the
imaginations of our poets at all, it has stirred
them in a different way. What good Christmas poetry we have is, most of it, stately and
magnificent, and like Handel's *Messiah*, concerned rather with the splendour and glorious
promise of the Nativity than with its mystery
and pathetic strangeness. Milton's Ode, for
instance, is finest in the prophecy of a golden
age to be, and in its exultation over the de-
thronement of pagan deities. The contrast
between the Godhead and its surrounding is
expressed in rather frigid and forced conceits.
There is no tenderness for the Divine Child, no
concern with the mystery of the Incarnation.
Milton, in fact, though it seems a bold thing
to say, had not a deep religious imagination.
It was never the essential part of a sacred

Crashaw's Christmas Poems

theme that inspired him, and his finest images illustrate not the nature but the accessories of Divinity. To him heaven is music and multitudes of glittering forms. His imagination never dwells upon its spiritual side. He is the most complete Ritualist, for all his Puritanism, of all religious poets. So he thought of the Nativity as a most important event to be celebrated in high ceremonial verse, as if he were the Poet Laureate of Christianity, and in the same spirit in which Virgil celebrated the coming birth of the unknown Infant who was to transform the world. There was nothing dramatic to him in the Nativity, no human interest, no pathos or strangeness; and his imagination never seized upon the essence of the situation, as it was seized by the imagination of a contemporary poet in those two verses :

That the Great Angel-blinding light should shrink
His blaze, to shine in a poor Shepherd's eye.
That the unmeasured God so low should sink,
As prisoner in a few poor rags to lie.
That from his Mother's Breast he milk should drink,
Who feeds with Nectar Heaven's fair family.
  That a vile Manger his low Bed should prove,
  Who on a Throne of stars Thunders above ;

That he whom the sun serves, should faintly peep
Through clouds of Infant flesh ; that he the old
Eternal Word should be a Child, and weep.
That he who made the fire, should fear the cold ;

3

More Essays on Religion

That Heaven's high Majesty his Court should keep
In a clay cottage, by each blast controlled.
    That Glory's self should serve our Griefs, and fears :
And free Eternity, submit to years.

These lines, unknown probably to many lovers
of poetry, are by Richard Crashaw, the most
neglected of our greatest poets. For he is a
great poet, and differs not in degree, but in
kind, from the many writers of a narrow perfection far better known to us. A few of his
inferior pieces are to be found in most antho-
logies. His best verses, like those just quoted,
are usually to be found in formless and unequal
poems; for his defects are as glaring as his
merits are splendid, and he very seldom
achieved a stately and connected whole. Yet
there is a deeper reason than these defects to
account for his neglect. The whole nature of
his religious emotion is strange to the English
mind. He became early in his short life a
Roman Catholic, and wrote of sacred subjects
rather like an Italian than an Englishman.
He was influenced, too, by Italian literature.
The " Sospetto d'Herode," from which the
verses quoted above are taken, is a free para-
phrase of a poem by Marino. Many English
poets of the sixteenth century were taken with
fantastic Italian conceits, but none were carried into such extravagances as Crashaw.
None certainly were, like him, filled with that

peculiar Italian religious feeling that is distasteful to most Englishmen. It is our habit to draw a strict line between our religious and other emotions, whereas the Italians of Crashaw's time found in their female saints a dangerous link between religion and erotics. In their religious art other passions sometimes seem to find a vent in pietistic ecstasy, and there is a taint of their sickly grossness in Crashaw's poetry. Sometimes he seems to take too physical a delight in themes that we associate only with the austerity of spiritual beauty. But these lapses are not frequent, and it is their unfamiliarity that makes them so disagreeable to us. The great mass of his religious poetry is wholesome enough, though its splendours are remote from our interest. His imagination was not concerned with the practice of religion, but with dazzling images of the mysteries of faith and with rapt expressions, almost pictorial in their vividness, of heavenly magnificence. He exults in images of the inscrutable glory of God. Like Correggio, he

Loves to mass, in rifts
Of heaven, his angel faces, orb on orb . . .
Waiting to see some wonder momently
Grow out, stand full, fade slow against the sky.

His verse is thronged with celestial ardour, and with celestial music too. Yet, though a

5

visionary poet, he is seldom vaporous. There is a certain definiteness in his images that gives substance to his most exalted raptures. Like most of the poets of his time, he loved " wit," and would apply it to the most imaginative subjects, sometimes disastrously, sometimes with the most splendid results. Wit is concrete in its essence, and its function is to illustrate abstractions by a surprising and concrete example. Often enough Crashaw used examples altogether too concrete. Homeliness is incongruous to the nature of his mind and to the splendid texture of his verse, and when in imitation of Donne and Herbert he tries to be homely, he is often exquisitely absurd. But in his happier moments he is our greatest master of imaginative epigram. Then he combines all the dilating vastness of poetry with the happy surprises and precise application of an epigram. There could not be a better subject for imaginative wit than the Incarnation, and it was natural that Crashaw should rise to his greatest heights in writing of it. Indeed the line

> And free Eternity, submit to years

is perhaps the finest poetic epigram in the language. It is the most splendid example of a kind of inspired wit almost lost to us. In the eighteenth century there was wit enough, but

little inspiration. In the nineteenth, plenty
of inspiration, but little wit. Never since the
seventeenth have the two been combined in
that surprising union. There is less wit, but
hardly less eloquence, in another verse in the
" Sospetto d'Herode."

He saw how in that blest Day-bearing Night,
The Heaven-rebuked shades made haste away ;
How bright a Dawn of Angels with new Light
Amazed the midnight world, and made a Day
Of which the Morning knew not : Mad with spite
He marked how the poor Shepherds ran to pay
  Their simple Tribute to the Babe, whose Birth
  Was the great business both of Heaven and Earth.

One may note here how curiously the two and
a half lines beginning " How bright a dawn of
angels " anticipate the lyric accent of Shelley.
There are other poems of Crashaw's that anticipate yet more strangely the most elaborate
effects of Swinburne.

Crashaw wrote also, in a more lyrical and
less weighty style, a Hymn of the Nativity,
sung by shepherds, Thyrsis answering to Tityrus with a curious mixture of sacred and
classical association that reminds one how the
Italian painters were eager to seize any excuse,
as in the frequent representation of St. Sebas-
tian, for imitating the antique in religious
pictures. The poem, of course, is very artificial in form and contains some monstrous
conceits. For this reason it is never likely to

be popular. Half the verses, at least, one could wish away; but the rest have a swift lyrical beauty, a richness and lightness of sound not heard in our poets before, and not to be heard again until the nineteenth century. Here is a verse, for instance, which both the shepherds sing:

> We saw thee in thy balmy nest,
> Bright dawn of our eternal Day!
> We saw thine eyes break from their East
> And chase the trembling shades away,
> We saw Thee, and we blest the sight;
> We saw Thee, by Thine own sweet light.

Here is part of another, sung by Tityrus:

> I saw the curled drops, soft and slow,
>   Come hovering o'er the place's head;
> Offering their whitest sheets of snow
>   To furnish the fair Infant's bed:

To which Thyrsis makes a more splendid reply:

> I saw the obsequious Seraphims
>   Their rosy fleece of fire bestow.
> For well they now can spare their wing
>   Since Heaven itself lies here below.

Crashaw has written other poems on Christmas themes. There is one on the Circumcision —a subject that tempts him into some rather forced conceits, though they are all expressed with great beauty of rhythm. He wrote, too, " An Address to the Queen's Majesty on

Twelfth Day," full of pompous and over-elaborate compliments with an almost blasphemous comparison between the royalites of the Queen and of the Infant Christ. Yet the opening is stately enough in all its exaggeration :

'Mongst those long rows of crowns that gild your race,
These royal sages sue for decent place.
The daybreak of the nations ; their first ray ;
When the Dark World dawned into Christian Day,
And smiled i' the Babe's bright face, the purpling Bud
And Rosy dawn of the right Royal blood.

But these verses ought perhaps to be placed among the curiosities rather than the beauties of literature, and still more ought the " Hymn as Sung by the Three Kings " for the Epiphany. It is an almost worthless poem of many pages, filled with one long-drawn comparison between the Infant Christ and the Sun. This is a comparison that Crashaw was never tired of, though it soon tires his readers. He is sometimes inclined to think that a religious poem requires no subject-matter except such comparisons. They prove the writer's piety, and nothing else is needed.

But that is enough of Crashaw's faults. They are illustrated well enough in his Christmas poetry ; and so are most of his merits, except perhaps the most remarkable of all, his extraordinary command of lyrical irregular verse. He was the first master of this and among the greatest that have ever practised it. In his hands it is an instrument on which every effect of majesty and swiftness, of delicacy and grandeur, can be produced at will. To prove this an extract must be taken, not from any of the Christmas pieces, but from the hymn to "The Name above every Name, the Name of Jesus," the finest of all his poems. At the very beginning of it occurs the address to the Saints and Martyrs:

> The Heirs Elect of Love; whose Names belong
> Unto The everlasting life of Song;

the second line of which is unsurpassed for its union of largeness and propriety of expression. About the middle of the poem is the following passage:

> May it be no wrong
> Blest Heavens, to you, and your Superior song,
> That we, dark Sons of Dust and Sorrow,
> Awhile Dare borrow
> The Name of Your Delights and our Desires,
> And fit it to so far inferior Lyres.
> Our Murmurs have their Music too,
> Ye Mighty Orbs, as well as you,
> Nor yields the noblest Nest
> Of warbling Seraphim to the ears of Love,
> A choicer Lesson than the joyful Breast
> Of a poor panting Turtle-Dove.

With which magnificent burst of varied music we commend Crashaw to the Christmas leisure of the reader.

Christina Rossetti ✐ ✐ ✐

THERE is nothing surprising in the facts of Christina Rossetti's life. Indeed, they are just what one would expect from her poetry. She lived a secluded life of devotion to her family, and particularly to her mother. The beautiful dedicatory sonnet to the volume of 1881 is only the poetic expression of a love that was the chief earthly business of her life. Her health was nearly always bad, and she suffered constantly. She was religious with a medieval intensity of belief and devotion. She was twice loved and in love, but refused to marry because in each case her lover's faith was different from her own. In the second case she continued to love the man she rejected until he died. Her religion, though it made her kind to others, did not make her kind to herself; nor did it make her happy. She was filled with an awful sense of unworthiness, shadowed by an awful uncertainty. In spite of her innocent life and all her religious exercises, she was always despondent of her own righteousness. These religious exercises and meditations and searchings of heart never distracted her from her ordinary duties, never soured her temper or unbalanced her mind ; but they were always the chief business of her life. One can imagine her calm and restrained in manner, talking or listening readily and without arrogance or affectation, yet always as if some one great interest possessed the depths of her mind and other things were but momentary distractions of the surface.

Her poetry confirms this idea of her. It has many subjects ; but all of them, except one, are transient and occasional. Her main and constant theme is the desire for a security of righteousness never attained. Her piety, her devotion to duty, her even and sequestered way of life could not protect her from the fever and unrest with which the desire for some kind of impossible perfection has afflicted so many poets. Usually that desire is only vague and occasional. Shelley was haunted by dreams of an ideal beauty, a perfect love. Even Browning had his moods of—

> Infinite passion and the pain
> Of finite hearts that yearn.

Matthew Arnold longed for some kind of certainty that life was not an aimless mechanical process. This disease of the poets has many forms. It lies in wait for them when they are overwrought; and Christina Rossetti, from her physical weakness, was constantly overwrought. It is clear from her life and her poetry that her mind was not naturally morbid. She shows a pathetic eagerness for simple and wholesome delights. But the poetic disease took so cunning a form in her that it enlisted all her finer qualities in its service. In most poets it is not encouraged by any creed or principles. In their healthier moods they are impatient of it. They see that it is irrational, and even when it troubles them most they try to reason it away. Christina Rossetti could not do this. Her longing for perfection, her desire for some kind of unearthly certainty seemed to her always right and reasonable, since they were inspired by her religion. She wished to love God perfectly and to be sure of her love; and she would have thought it impious to reason with her misgivings about it. The natural despondency produced by her physical weakness always oppressed her with a sense of her own imperfections; and as she thought that this sense was justified she could only meet the despondency by continually assuring herself that God was right to afflict her so. One can see in her poetry that she was for ever straining after the exultant raptures of the saints and for ever breaking down under

the strain. The artistic temperament may be
directed by religion ; it cannot be changed, as
George Herbert proved long ago. It makes
its own joys and sorrows, and feeds upon itself.
It is eager for delight, expects impatiently, and
remembers mournfully its rare moments of
confident exultation ; and aggravates its moods
of flat despondency by futile rebellion against
them.

> Rarely, rarely, comest thou,
> Spirit of Delight,

cried Shelley in unreasoning complaint. Christina Rossetti sometimes utters the same
cry :

How tired a face, how tired a brain, how tired
A heart I lift, who long
For something never felt but still desired ;
Sunshine and song.
Song where the Choirs of sunny Heaven stand choired.

Yet she upbraids herself for uttering it.

> Alas thou foolish one ! Alike unfit
> For healthy joy and salutary pain :
> Thou knowest the chase useless, and again
> Turnest to follow it.

She contends bravely with her despondencies,
but cannot master them. She looks back
mournfully to the past as a time when she was
good herself and assured of the goodness of
God :

Christina Rossetti

> Lord, it was well with me in time gone by
> That cometh not again,
> When I was fresh and cheerful.

Like Herbert, she treasures up her moments of happy reaction from hours of darkness :

> Thy promise stands, Thou Faithful One,
> Horror of Darkness disappeared
> At length : once more I see the sun,
> And dare to wait in hope for spring.

Compare these lines from Herbert's " Flower " :

> I once more smell the dew and rain,
> And relish versing : O my only light,
> It cannot be
> That I am he,
> On whom Thy tempests fell at night.

The moods of the two poets are often alike. Both are troubled by the insecurity of their spiritual raptures. Herbert writes :

How should I praise Thee, Lord, how should my
> rhymes
> Gladly engrave Thy Love in steel,
If what my soul doth feel sometimes
> My soul might ever feel.

And Christina Rossetti says :

> It seems an easy thing
> Mayhap one day to sing ;
> Yet the next day
> We cannot sing or say.

Both of them see in this insecurity a proof that their love of God is imperfect :

More Essays on Religion

> I love and love not : Lord, it breaks my heart
>   To love and not to love.
> Thou veiled within Thy glory, gone apart
>   Into Thy shrine which is above,
> Dost Thou not love me, Lord, or care
>   For this mine ill ?

Both of them are for ever seeking to justify the ways of God to themselves. They must convince themselves that God is good. They cry to Him to solve their doubts :

> Now I would stay ; God bids me go :
> Now I would rest ; God bids me work.
> He breaks my heart tossed to and fro,
>   My soul is wrung with doubts that lurk
>   And vex it so.

They can believe without question ; but they cannot love without question. Their reason is obedient, but not their emotions. They cannot always feel the goodness of God, and they are for ever straining themselves to feel it. If they felt the goodness of God, they argue, they would be happy ; they are not happy ; therefore, they do not feel it. Like all poets, they will not understand that happiness cannot be ensured by any effort however strong, by any passion however lofty or intense. Like all poets, they are hungry for delight, and that hunger is the cause of half their miseries. With the best will in the world they cannot be content with the conditions of

16

Christina Rossetti

life as they are. Knowing that it is wrong to pine for earthly pleasures, they pine for celestial ; and impute it to their own wicked- ness when they cannot attain to them.

The most frequent of Christina Rossetti's themes is the longing for heaven as a place where all her misgivings will be quieted and where all imperfect terrestrial delights of eye and ear and heart will be made perfect. It is one of the chief subjects of all poetry, taking different forms according to the form of the poet's belief. It was the theme of Sophocles' old age in the " Œdipus Coloneus," of Shelley's " Prometheus Unbound," of Milton's " Blest Pair of Sirens," of Browning's " Prospice," and of many other masterpieces. But no poet has treated it so constantly or with such pathetic insistence as Christina Rossetti. Often prevented by distress of mind and body from taking pleasure in the precarious delights of this world, she got what consolation she could from imagining the sure and everlasting delights of another. There is a tremulous in- security about her dreams of heaven very different from the splendid certainties of Milton's vision. He writes of Paradise as if he were gazing steadfastly upon it as his own sure inheritance ; she as if she dared not raise her eyes to look upon glories she scarcely ventured to hope for, *insuetum miratur limen Olympi.*

More Essays on Religion

As I lie dreaming
　　It rises, that land ;
There rises before me
　　Its green golden strand,
With the bowing cedars
　　And the shining sand ;
It sparkles and flashes
　　Like a shaken brand.

But, after another verse she falls to thinking of the vanity of this life :

Oh what is a king here,
　　Or what is a boor ?
Here all starve together,
　　All dwarfed and poor ;
Here Death's hand knocketh
　　At door after door,
He thins the dancers
　　From the festal floor.

And the poem ends in a cry of vanity of vanities. The moods of her more secular poems are much the same. Death is a constant theme, and love is only something that might have been or may be in another world :

O dream how sweet, too sweet, too bitter sweet,
　　Whose wakening should have been in Paradise,
Where souls brimfull of love abide and meet ;
　　Where thirsting, longing eyes
　　　　Watch the slow door
That opening, letting in, lets out no more.

Yet this mournful music expresses not the luxury of a fanciful melancholy, but the real pangs of a woman who had forgone love from

18

Christina Rossetti

a sense of duty.   There is no literary insincerity in Christina Rossetti's poetry.   It is full of brave efforts to be cheerful, though many things justified her sadness.   It is clear that she felt the want of the love she had denied herself all through her life ; and her celestial yearnings were often perhaps only the unconscious expression of that want.   She enjoys the beauties of the earth and sky always with a sense of their precariousness and with the faint delight of one who feels the wind and sun for the first time after a long sickness—

> All the world is out in leaf,
>   Half the world in flower,
> Earth has waited weeks and weeks
>   For this special hour :
> Faint the rainbow comes and goes
>   On a sunny shower.

Yet, even when she begins a poem gaily, she can seldom continue gay to the end of it. There is a note of anxiety in her most cheerful verses, and she seems to watch over the young girls of her narrative poems with the anxiety of a mother troubled by her children's happiness because she has learnt to distrust life herself.

It would be idle to expect from a poet of this kind the triumphant richness of balanced passion, delight, and power.   Christina Rossetti's verse does not move with the confident swiftness, the exultant majesty, of the greatest lyric poets. She had no overplus of strength to spend in lavish imagery or to kindle her thoughts with the heat of their own upward rush. Passion always overstrained her, and the strain can be felt in the very structure of her verse. Yet, though overstrained, she is never overblown like Mrs. Browning, who aimed often at the large manner of strong masculine poets and attained it only in a few masterpieces. These are beyond the reach of Christina Rossetti, but she had a surer though a quieter magic of her own. Her voice is very pure, if sometimes weak and thin ; and it is full of a most moving, unforced tenderness. It is natural to speak of her voice, for it seems to sound in her verses—and it is not common for poets, even great ones, to produce that illusion, since the combination of quick emotion with perfect sincerity and simplicity of mind is not common. She had a fine though narrow command of rhythm. In some of her slow lyrics the words seem to be falling naturally from her lips, urged by passion and checked by thought. Some poets, like Swinburne, seem to have all their rhythmical effects dictated by the metre of their choice. They look to the metre itself to suggest its own variations or even occasional divergencies from it. They work always upon a preordained pattern which masters all diversities of emotion with its persistent recurrence. The rhythmical effects of Christina Rossetti, except in some of her earlier poems, such as " Dreamland " and " When I am dead, my dearest," seem rather to be dictated by the sense. There is a metre, but she is not concerned to keep time with it. The beat is broken by long pauses, hesitations of thought, quick rushes of emotion. The metrical scheme itself is irregular so that it may never become insistent and all obvious cadences are avoided. The rhymes only answer each other like the faint echoes which all great masters of verbal music introduce irregularly into their lines ; they do not mark a period either of rhythm or of sense.

This way of writing was the result, no doubt, of the scrupulous probity of her art. She distrusted the charms of obvious rhythm, because they are apt to tempt the poet to say more than he feels. The regular beat may work him into a spurious frenzy, like the tom-toms of a barbaric dance ; the formal cadences may take the place of an orator's tricks of voice and gesture. Wordsworth himself was not more careful to avoid oratorical insincerities than Christina Rossetti. She never feigned a lyric gusto which she did not feel. She was content to speak when a connexion of sense was necessary in the pauses of her natural song,

and there are many bald passages in her poetry
which any fluent versemaker could enrich.
But even these have their artistic value; for
they persuade the reader to trust her, to accept
her music, when it comes, with unquestioning
delight, and to believe that the wonders of her
thought are the experiences of real adventures
of the mind. We may wish that her mind had
met with happier adventures, had strengthened
and eased itself more by disinterested contem-
plation of the spectacle of life. It is natural
to feel some impatience over the painful
introspection of poets, and to wonder why
more of them do not try to set the simple joy
of living to music. We have real troubles
enough of our own without being lured by art
to listen to outcries of what is often only the
pain of the mere process of thought. Yet we
should remember that the poet's thought is
apt to be painful because his body takes its
revenge for the exactions of his imperious
mind. Poets are all too eager for the joy of
life. They lie in wait for it, and vex themselves with perverse reasonings when it eludes
them. There is something of the poet's per-
versity in Christina Rossetti's sorrow; yet we
cannot be impatient with it, because it is so
clearly the weakness of a mind that exacts too
much, not of life, but of itself. She had not
the power of the greatest poets to draw the

mind out of itself into a world of its own invention. She could not create tragic figures to bear the burden of her own sorrow. She could not breathe life into a Hamlet, or stand aloof smiling while he gave utterance to the irrational misgivings of her own darker moods. She could only express her own moods, dark or shining, as they came to her. But the expression of them ought to touch us like the outcries of the hero of a moving play, drawn from him by an adverse fate. Indeed, in her poetry there is the long and quiet tragedy of a mind too aspiring and a body too frail for the conditions of our life, yet struggling bravely, if often blindly, against them ; and the tragedy is lightened with many intervals of innocent delight and snatches of clear music :

> Sing in the silent sky,
>   Glad soaring bird ;
> Sing out thy notes on high
> To sunbeam straying by
> Or passing cloud ;
>   Heedless if thou art heard,
> Sing thy full song aloud.

III

The Rev. Robert Herrick ✑ ✑

THE poetry of Herrick is more interesting and more read than much more ambitious and highly praised poetry because it is full of his own experience. For this reason he might be read with pleasure by those who do not care for poetry at all, but who do care for human nature. You may forget that he is a poet and regard him as a kind of Pepys who kept a versified diary, not in chronological order, and mainly about his sensations and emotions. He seems to write, not for publication, but because he likes to express himself. He never has the air of saying more than he feels, never tries to make himself out a finer fellow than he is. Though he plays a beautiful and elaborate game of verse, he plays it, like patience, all by himself and without any consciousness of an audience. Reading him, you remember that he wrote far away in his Devonshire vicarage, where his poems were the events of his life. They have a sequestered and provincial air. There are only memories of the town in them, which had become a distant romance for him ; and in their literary fashion they belong to the past. Herrick has been called a belated Elizabethan, and he was certainly not in the movement of the seventeenth century. He looks back to the Mermaid and the old songs that were made to be sung. But he keeps to the past because he is cut off from the present, not because he is dull ; and it was lucky for his art that he was cut off from the present. The fantastic poetry of the time, which he might have tried to write if he had lived in London, is good only in heaven-sent moments, though then it is magnificent. The kind of Elizabethan poetry that Herrick wrote does not need heaven-sent moments, because it does not pretend to treat of great matters. It was the product of an age in which so many people wrote verse for their own pleasure that no versifier was tempted to give himself the airs of a poet. Nowadays a poet is a peculiar person at whom the world is apt to laugh ; so the minor poet makes the most of his peculiarity, and pretends to all the passions of the great one. But in the age of Elizabeth writing verses was a game as common and as much respected as golf is now ; and the amateur versifier could play it without any self-consciousness. The great mass of Elizabethan lyrics are good because they do not attempt

3

to be too good. They express ordinary emotions without trying to make them seem extraordinary, and with a skill that came of general practice. Thus, if we make too much of them we miss the point of them altogether. Even Shakespeare in his songs usually writes like the ordinary amateur of the time, only better. He does not attempt the passion or subtlety of later lyric poets, but composes words for music just like Campion or any other gifted versifier.

Herrick carried on this tradition in his own country isolation; but he surpassed the ordinary Elizabethan song-writer not only in technique but in the range of his subjects. The great defects of Elizabethan lyrics, for the modern reader, are emptiness and monotony. We have no right to complain of this, for they were made to be sung, not read; and when we read them in the mass we are maltreating them. But Herrick meant many of his verses to be read; and his great achievement was the application of the Elizabethan lyrical manner to a new subject-matter. The Elizabethan song-writers wrote generalities. They made songs that any lover might sing to his mistress—standardized songs, as we should say. Herrick kept their clearness of music, but he wrote about himself and his own peculiar feelings and affairs with the same freedom from

The Rev. Robert Herrick

strain and solemn airs, the same easy avoidance of prosaic or dowdy language. In his poetry there is not only music but character; and that is what makes it interesting as well as beautiful. He is not merely a belated Elizabethan, but the first poet of the age of reason, and the best of them all. He could have taught many lessons to the versifiers of the eighteenth century and even to Pope. In particular he could have taught them how to be homely but not prosaic; how to put precise detail in verse without jarring upon either its music or its mood. He could have told them the great secret, which they never knew, that the purpose of generalization in poetry is to express passion, not to conceal the want of it. The famous Night Piece begins full of detail, though it is one of his most lyrical poems:

> Her eyes the glow-worm lend thee,
> The shooting stars attend thee;
>   And the Elves also,
>   Whose little eyes glow,
> Like the sparks of fire, befriend thee.

But gradually the detail is more and more lost in the music, and the last verse is nearly all tune:

> Then, Julia, let me woo thee,
> Thus, thus, to come unto me;
>   And when I shall meet
>   Thy silv'ry feet
> My soul I'll pour into thee.

More Essays on Religion

This poem is very like an Elizabethan song ; but what a world of its own it makes, a world which, no doubt, Herrick created in his mind upon his lonely evening walks, imagining a human romance that he was never to enjoy, to fit all the scents and sounds of a starry summer night. It must have been this kind of imagining that made him half hate and half love the country. It was a beautiful setting for the life of his dreams, but there he was alone in it, with absurd duties to perform among barbarians, and only able to live his real life in his poetry :

> More discontents I never had
>   Since I was born, than here ;
> Where I have been, and still am sad,
>   In this dull Devonshire ;
> Yet justly too I must confess ;
>   I ne'er invented such
> Ennobled numbers for the Press,
>   Than where I loathed so much.

If he had been a man about town, he might have turned into a mere idler listening to the talk of Ben Jonson ; or he might have caught the new fashion of fantastic poetry that could never have suited his genius. But in Devonshire he remained hungry for imagined triumphs of love and art, and out of these he made real triumphs. There was not a soul, perhaps, to assure him that they were triumphs, so he

The Rev. Robert Herrick

assured himself in verses which themselves approved his claim :

> Behold this living stone,
>   I rear for me,
>   Ne'er to be thrown
> Down, envious Time, by thee.
>
> Pillars let some set up
>   (If so they please).
> Here is my hope,
>   And my Pyramides.

Though so few certain facts are known about Herrick, it is not difficult to imagine the kind of life he led or the manner in which his mind worked. He must have been a man with some dangerous and exorbitant desires, which he could satisfy, or at least mitigate, by making verses about them. If he had not had that wonderful natural gift, he might have gone to the bad ; but his gift enabled him to escape into a world of pure mind where those desires were all harmless. He could not have been satisfied with that world if it had existed only in vague dreams ; but when he wrote poetry he passed from dreams to action. He accomplished something and became a triumphant poet if not a triumphant lover. But this world of his which he made in the Hesperides is interesting to us because so many facts connect it with real life. He had as great a zest for actual things as Pepys himself. He could enjoy his hatreds and take a private revenge upon the Philistines about him in coarse epigrams which, very likely, they never read.

First, Jollie's wife is lame; then next, loose hipt: Squint-eyed, hook-nosed; and lastly, kidney-lipt.

That reads like a note upon a real woman; and here again is a note of a different kind made both musical and vivid with his peculiar art:

> Dew sate on Julia's hair,
>   And spangled too,
> Like Leaves that laden are
>   With trembling Dew;
> Or glittered to my sight,
>   As when the Beams
> Have their reflected light
>   Danced by the Streams.

No other poet with such powers is so completely satisfied with the object or the moment described. His method is the opposite of Donne's, whose realism is employed only to heighten the wonder of his escape into infinity. For Herrick, there is no such thing as infinity, no baffling significance in the beauty of real things. He asks no questions about it, but enjoys it as a child enjoys flowers or sweets. The images in this little poem are employed only to emphasize what delights him in the thing seen. He uses the method of agreement for artistic purposes; and he is an artist because he can express his delights in the music of his words. In fact the poem is an æsthetic document, just because it does so little and yet satisfies ; it throws more light upon the nature of poetry than poems which appeal to the heart or the intellect. You may be bewildered by the larger powers and interest of other poets, so that you think your enjoyment of them is æsthetic when it is not ; but your enjoyment of this poem and of many others which Herrick wrote can be only æsthetic. In them he expresses and communicates just the emotion which he experienced himself and nothing else.

He could not have done this without remarkable sincerity ; and that is the only moral quality that we discover in him. But it is the one moral quality necessary to an artist. Herrick, in his art at least, was the most honest of men. He is less plausible even than Wordsworth, for Wordsworth could be pompous ; but Herrick could not. That is the reason why we can all take his poetry as he asks the generous reader to take it.

See, and not see ; and if thou chance t' espy
Some Aberrations in my Poetry ;
Wink at small faults, the greater, ne'rtheless
Hide, and with them, their Father's nakedness.
Let's do our best, our Watch and Ward to keep :
Homer himself, in a long work, may sleep.

One would expect such a poet to fail utterly

if he attempted religious verse. But Herrick is preserved by his sincerity from disaster, even in his "pious pieces," for he never pretends to more piety than he feels. He is just as unconscious of an audience in them as in his love poems. He writes like a layman, not like a parson; indeed, the Noble Numbers show us more clearly even than the Hesperides how little he kept his parishioners in mind. He is never so pagan as when he is devout; for religion to him is only a means of living happily. He ought, one feels, to have been a Roman Catholic of South Italy with a multitude of saints to pray to. He could have written verses to them all as to his multitude of imaginary mistresses; and they would have made life more amusing and comfortable for him. His kind of religion has almost disappeared now in England, and it was disappearing in his own time even, as the Puritans grew stronger. They would certainly have thought his Thanksgiving for his House blasphemous in its triviality:

> Lord, 'tis thy plenty-dropping hand,
> That soiles my land;
> And giv'st me, for my Bushell sown,
> Twice ten for one;
> Thou mak'st my teeming Hen to lay
> Her egg each day.

There is just the same comfortable satisfaction

32

The Rev. Robert Herrick

in this as in the secular poem to his brother on
a country life :

Yet can thy humble roof maintain a Quire
Of singing Crickets by thy fire ;
And the brisk Mouse may feast herself with crumbs,
Till that the green-eyed Kitling comes ;
Then to her Cabin, blest she can escape
The sudden danger of a Rape.
And thus thy little-well-kept-stock doth prove,
Wealth cannot make a life, but Love.

These last two lines might be a motto for all
Herrick's poetry.   He must have loved a great
many things quite disinterestedly.   He may
have wished for worldly success and the pleasures of town ; but the effectual part of his
mind exercised itself in the expression of his
love, and so his little stock of poetic power was
well kept.   Patmore called him a splendid in-
sect ; but he made too much of a home for
himself in the world to be that ; and he is more
even than a pleasant cricket chirping on the
hearth.   He had in his pocket a lonely flute
which he took out when he went abroad.   Then
he was transformed into the Eternal Shepherd,
whose song has sounded in so many tongues
and for so many ages, but never more purely
than when he sang it :

Ye have been fresh and green,
  Ye have been filled with flowers :
And ye the Walks have been
  Where Maids have spent their hours,

33

More Essays on Religion

You have beheld how they
  With Wicker Arks did come
To kiss, and bear away
  The richer Cowslips home.

Y'ave heard them sweetly sing,
  And seen them in a Round :
Each Virgin, like a Spring,
  With Honey-suckles crowned.

That music of his still haunts the meadows
round his parsonage and indeed all the meadows of England, so that they are enchanted
like the places where Sicilian shepherds sang.

I V

Ecclesiastical Art   ∽   ∽   ∽

THE GOTHIC AND THE GOOD

IT is often said that in the Middle Ages art was the handmaid of religion. But that is not quite true. They were on equal terms because art was the medium in which religion naturally expressed itself. Now it is not the medium in which religion expresses itself; and there is a desire to make it the handmaid of religion. The result is " ecclesiastical art," an art which is not free and therefore expresses nothing.

The clergy, and the devout laity, have the notion that art to be religious must be archaistic. Gothic art, they think, is religious art; but no art, now, is naturally Gothic; and so this Gothic religious art of theirs is not art— that is to say, it is not expressive. Modern Gothic, as it is practised in churches, is all a matter of ornament, or pinnacles and cusps and crockets and window tracery. These things seem to the devout religious. Without them a church would not seem a church at all; and an altar would not be an altar without an altar-cloth worked with dull, rigid embroideries, such as no one would tolerate in a drawing-room. The standard for ecclesiastical art is different in kind from the standard for art, because religion is supposed to express itself artistically in a style which no artist now practises naturally.

Hence most ecclesiastical art is purely commercial and supplied by " firms " whose artistic standard is lower than that of the ordinary cheap furniture shop. And this commercial art is the negation, not only of art, but also of religion. The furniture of a church should be the best possible ; and religion expresses itself naturally in the desire to have the best in its places of worship. But in our places of worship, of all denominations, we have the worst ; because we suppose that religion expresses itself in a style, and we do not ask whether an object in that style is beautiful or ugly, well or ill made, whether in fact we like it. We assume that it is religious because it is in the religious style.

So, if art is again to become a natural expression of religion, we must get rid of ecclesiastical art in our churches. We must aim, not at the Gothic, but at the good. And we shall understand what the good is only if we cease to think of religious art as a matter of ornament,

Ecclesiastical Art

The good in art is, in the first place, that which is well designed for its purpose and made of good materials ; and religion expresses itself first in art by the desire to have everything in a church of the best. Therefore the furniture of our churches should be, not Gothic furniture, but the best furniture possible ; and the church itself should be, not Gothic, but the best building we can design for purposes of worship. We may make up our minds to the fact that we are not good now at designing ornament. We shall become good at it only when we have learnt to design structure well. Therefore we should make a beginning in religious art by designing the structure of our churches, and by building them as well as we can, and without any ornament whatsoever. A plain whitewashed room, now, if well-designed and well-built, is far more likely to be religious than a modern Gothic church with its toyshop ornaments. There is in bare spaces a humility and a simplicity that express the religious attitude and induce the religious mood ; whereas the toyshop ornaments, like the platitudes of religious jargon, merely weary and distract. It is not that all religious art is necessarily bare and simple. It is that we need now to begin again at the beginning, which is good design and good workmanship. When we have recovered these, we may rise to ornament really expressive of our own religious emotions.

To take a particular instance—the altar is a table, and in our churches it should be the best table possible. Its cloth should be the best tablecloth possible, not an ecclesiastical cloth. If there are candlesticks on it, they should be the best candlesticks, not Gothic candlesticks so ugly that no one would endure them in his own house. If there are flowers in vases, the vases should be the most beautiful that can be obtained, not ecclesiastical vases that would shame a lodging-house mantelpiece ; and the flowers should be chosen and arranged for them as one would choose and arrange flowers in a room, only with more care and delight in their beauty. Then the altar, since it would express a real sense of beauty, a real desire for the best, and a real delight in it, would be really religious. We all feel the touching beauty of an old village church, and that is not because it is Gothic, but because it is the simple best of those who built it. But there is no beauty in the modern altars and ornaments of most village churches. They seem to be merely inadequate make-shifts, because they express nothing except a desire to follow a stale ecclesiastical fashion. They are both tawdry and bleak, like the ornaments of an unsuccessful hotel.

If any clergyman tried to furnish his church

Ecclesiastical Art

according to his own idea of what was beautiful, if he treated his altar as we have suggested, his congregation would probably think they were shocked. But they would not really be shocked ; and they would soon become inured to beauty even in church. It is of some importance that their prejudices should be overcome, so that we may begin to have a real religious art again ; and no amount of talking will overcome them. The clergy must be brave, learn to see in ecclesiastical art an expression of commercial atheism, and try to make their churches beautiful according to their own ideas of beauty. They will make mistakes no doubt ; but they will be nothing to the mistakes they make now.

There is a language in great architecture, as in music, which all can understand if they have the chance of listening to it. It is a common mistake of the Church to suppose that these things speak only to experts or connoisseurs, that in matters of art the mass of men like what is bad and must be given it, so that they may be tempted into church. Even if this were true, the Church has no more right to give them bad art because they like it than to give them bad morals because they like them. Art can be religious only if it is good. But we do not believe that the mass of men prefer bad art. It is true that they often like bad hymns because they are used to them ; but they would like good hymns better if they were used to them. They do like the tune of *Adeste Fideles* as well as any tune, and nothing could be better than that.

In such matters the Church has long been too kindly and too complaisant. It has appealed to the weakness rather than to the strength of Churchmen. It did not do this in its great days of creative art. Then it made the demand for great art by its supply ; now it tries to supply an answer to what it supposes to be a low demand. And so it is assumed that visitors to a cathedral cannot understand the music of the great building unless the history of it is explained to them. But this music spoke in the past to crowds of unlettered worshippers. The great cathedrals were built because people wanted them, and they wanted them because they were used to them. The supply of all the glorious art of the Middle Ages made the demand, but the demand was a fact, and it was made by our own forefathers, by men just like ourselves. It is time that in all matters of art the Church should be brave ; that it should not cast about to discover what the public wants, but should give the public its best both for eye and ear, and should have faith that the public will prefer its best to its worst.

Ecclesiastical Art

A beginning would be made if the cathedrals came to life again, if they became homes for the people where they might sit and learn the nature of silent and individual worship from the beauty of the place.   Then there might be a slow, steady effort to give good hymns instead of bad ones, both words and tunes.   Then altars might be made simple and beautiful and less like stalls at a bazaar.   In time a great deal of modern trash might be swept away, even from cathedral choirs.   Our way to the expression of religion in art must be through good material, good workmanship, and the plainest possible design.   If people complain of this at first, let them have time to get used to it.   They do not want trash in a mission room ; why should they want it in a cathedral ?   The Gothic style, both in building and in furniture, has become merely a bad habit with the Church.   People think they like it because they are used to it, just as they think they like bad German hymn tunes and worse English imitations of them.   But it is impossible that they should really like such things, or the Gothic candlesticks commonly seen on altars, or the lecterns and pulpits and reredoses. What they do like is the associations which have gathered round those things.   This is a pathetic fact, and it will no doubt cause some pain to break with such associations ; but it must be done if religion is to speak again with all its voices. The Church must not be æsthetically disreputable, any more than it must intellectually contemptible ; for religion can only speak to the senses with the voice of beauty.

When the voice of ugliness is heard it is not religion that speaks at all. Devils are not to be cast out with the help of devils, and bad art, most of all when it is an imitation of good, comes from Satan. Bad art may be liked for its associations or for what it pretends to be ; but good art can only be loved for itself : and we believe it can still be loved by all men ; we believe that a great building can speak to them without explanations ; that great music can stir them as it stirred their forefathers. It is time that the Church believed this and acted upon its belief.

V

" Restoration and Renovation " ᴑ

THERE are still many people who do not
see why we should not " restore " old
Gothic buildings, why we should not
have modern imitative Gothic, why we should
not have imitative art of any kind. I often
talk to people on that subject, try to argue
with them, and often I find that I cannot begin
to make an impression. I have the same effect
upon them that people have on me who try to
explain Einstein. I have no doubt that here [1]
we all agree on the subject, but I think we want
reasons for our faith ; for one thing so that we
may propagate it, and for another because,
without reasons, your faith is not firmly estab-
lished in your own mind. If you hold a belief
for which you cannot give reasons, so that you
are merely angry if anybody contests it—then
you hold that belief insecurely, and your very
anger is a symptom of fear lest it might be
undermined. Therefore I will try to give
reasons for my belief that you cannot have
imitative art.

[1] This paper was read to the Society for the Protection
of Ancient Buildings, June 14th, 1922.

43

I meet people who say that they cannot see why a copy of a picture should not be as good as the picture itself. It may be exactly like it ; the copyist can take his brush and, if he is skilful enough, he can copy the original stroke by stroke. I think one can put the answer scientifically. Only the same cause can produce the same effect, and if you start copying a picture your process is different from the process of the original artist. You are trying to make your picture as like his as possible, but he was not trying to make his like another picture. Therefore the strokes which you, the copyist, put on your canvas cannot be like the strokes which he put on his. They may *look* alike to anybody who looks at them in detail ; but the true test is this : Is there or is there not a difference in the *feeling* which the two pictures produce ? You should say to yourself not, " When I look at those two pictures do they seem to me exactly alike ? " but, " Do I feel alike when I look at them ? " That is the real test, and that is the scientific test ; because we must finally judge works of art by the feeling or emotion which they produce in us. That is our instinctive judgment, our right judgment, and better than the judgment based on minute observation of particulars.

Now in imitative restoration or imitative Gothic of any kind, the case is just the same as

" Restoration and Renovation "

in the case of copying a picture. The impulse
of imitative architecture is different from the
impulse of the original, because the original
architect was not trying to make his building
as much like another building as he could,
whereas the imitative architect is trying to
make his as much like another building, or at
least as much like another style, as he can. If
the impulse, the cause, is different, the result
will be different ; and though the two things
may seem to your eye very much alike, to your
mind they will be utterly different because
they will produce utterly different feelings.
There are experts in different arts whose business it is to know forgeries from originals ; and it
is a curious fact that the most learned experts—
not charlatans at all but very learned men—are
often taken in by forgeries. Why was it that
Herr Bodë bought, as by Leonardo, a bust by
a gentleman called Lucas, done in the reign of
Queen Victoria ? It was because his business
was to know whether works of art were genuine. By the very fact that he was always
looking at minute particulars in the work of art,
he was cut off from the only kind of æsthetic
experience which would enable him to tell
whether it was a forgery or not. The only
final test, the test which must baffle the skill of
the forger, is the test of feeling. All forgeries,
we may say, if they are only forgeries, must be

dull, because their impulse is not the impulse that produces works of art. No doubt things which are not forgeries are dull too : but, if a man resolved that he would have nothing to do with things that seemed to him dull, he would never be taken in by a forgery. It is because experts look at details all the time that they are cut off from the only æsthetic experience which would enable them to know a genuine work of art. It is because people look at details only in buildings, because the clergy often learn to recognize style, and are pleased when they can say that a building is Early English, or what not, that they are cut off from the only kind of experience which would enable them to know whether it was expressive building. Architecture is a language, a mode of expression ; and so if a building gives you that peculiar feeling of dullness, of mustiness, of being unable to believe in anything whatever, which is produced by, say, Worcester Cathedral in its present condition, then you may be sure that, no matter how much it seems like the real thing, it is not the real thing.

I think that, in all matters of art, what we have got to learn first of all is to identify our feelings, to be fully aware of them. We have got the notion that our feelings are necessarily vague because we cannot always express them precisely in language ; but the expression of feelings, of emotions, in terms of art, whether that art be music, painting or architecture—that expression is extremely precise, more precise indeed than our expression of intellectual concepts in words. We cannot perhaps state precisely in words what we feel, yet the feeling itself may be precise, and our understanding of the feeling may be precise ; nor can there be any æsthetic judgment of any value unless it is based on precise feeling.

Further, you must feel the beauty of great architecture if you are to see the dreariness of sham architecture. You must feel the beauty of Chartres if you are going to see the dreariness of Worcester. If you do not see the beauty of the real thing, you cannot see the dullness of the sham. I like to tell people this in the hope that I may arouse a conviction of sin in them. And, if once they grasp the fact that if you imitate anything you will fail to imitate the art in it, they will grasp also the great truth that any kind of architecture will go with real Gothic—except sham Gothic. It is a curious paradox that, in the effort to make our churches congruous, we have produced the one style that will not go with any style—that is, imitative Gothic. All styles that are genuine will go together. If Bernini had been turned into Durham Cathedral, he would have produced something far more congruous with the rest—

even if it had been like the Baldachino in St. Peter's—than the present screen ; for he would have expressed some feeling of his own, whereas the present screen expresses no feeling whatever.   There is curious proof of this in a tomb in York Minster—I think it is the tomb of Archbishop Gray—early Gothic, about 1220. It is a very charming tomb, and the finials at the top of it had been damaged ; so, about 1820, an Italian sculptor finished the finials in stucco.   You would not expect this to succeed, but it does.   The man did not care a scrap about Gothic or any style, but he thought it a beautiful tomb, and he made a design of his own to finish it ; and the effect is charming. He was an original artist ; he had no purpose of imitation, but he had an inspiration how to mend the tomb ; and it is the most successful piece of restoration I have ever seen, because it bears no possible resemblance to the original.

I dare not advise, I confess, for practical reasons, the clergy, architects, or general public to act on that principle, but theoretically I am sure it is right ; and practically whatever it produced would be better than imitative restoration.   I do not care what vulgarity is produced—I go as far as that—frank vulgarity would be better than mere imitation.   If it produced vulgarities instead of gentilities—and I think vulgarities better than gentilities—it

would be leading somewhere, whereas the
imitation of Gothic leads nowhere. It cuts the
architect off from the whole of that future
which he might enter into. Gothic, I am convinced, is now simply a bad habit, and it is a
bad habit encouraged by the clergy because
they think it religious. They have identified
the Gothic style with the Christian religion in
some mysterious way—perhaps they suppose
the early Christians built in Gothic, and they do
not realize that nothing can be less religious
than a style which is mere imitation. It is like
their unfortunate practice in the making of
new prayers, which are usually a patchwork
of phrases from old ones. You cannot pray
really in a patchwork of phrases ; nor can you
worship in a church which is a patchwork of
old details imitated from a style, possibly the
greatest that ever existed, but now obsolete.
I do not mean obsolete in a bad sense, but for
better or worse it is no longer a style in which
we naturally speak. So I believe—and I think
this ought to appeal to the clergy—that sham
Gothic architecture is a hindrance to religious
belief. For, with every impulse to expression,
if the expression fails, we actually become that
failure ; we become ourselves what we mis-
express ; and I am convinced that if you
worship in a church which is sham Gothic, the
prayers and the service will be infected by

association with the unreality of the building. I know that is so with regard to myself. If I hear a curate saying prayers as though neither he nor anybody else could believe them, I cease to believe—for the time, at any rate ; because his mis-expression makes his state of mind, and mine, that unreality which it expresses.

THE EVIL OF MIS-EXPRESSION

It is a fact about human beings that, if they mis-express themselves, they become that mis-expression. The most striking instance of that fact is the singing of cockneys ; they actually work themselves into a state of mind which fits their musical mis-expression. You know what I mean ; that shame-faced sneering at everything beautiful ; that half-comic, half-sentimental, drawl and drone. That is not what they start with the intention of doing, but it comes of their incapacity to express themselves ; their failure becomes their mood. That is why expression of all kinds is so important ; and not least in church architecture. If you habitually worship in a church which is sham Gothic, your religion will become sham Gothic itself. It will have the same taint of unreality. Further, sham Gothic is itself actually a symptom of something unreal in our religion. If that was perfectly genuine, we should not be able to endure a sham religious

expression; and if the clergy were aware of
that, instead of insisting upon sham Gothic as
being religious, they would demand rather even
a pretence of originality as being religious.
They would see that blatant vulgarity is better
than gentility because gentility is suppressed
vulgarity. Our modern Gothic reminds me of
the genteel manners of people out to tea and
uneasy because they do not know how to hold
their teacups. It is more Gothic than real
Gothic; just as people who are not quite sure
about their aitches put them in where they
are not wanted. That kind of gentility I con-
tend is worse than frank vulgarity, and I would
rather have the vulgarity of churches in Italy
—I go as far as that—than our sham Gothic
in England. That vulgarity is not suppressed
—anybody can see how blatant it is. Nobody
can pretend it is not as bad as it can be. It
is much harder to convert people from gentility
than from vulgarity, because they think it is
the right thing; I know it is very difficult to
convert people from sham Gothic; and I am
not as hopeful as the Chairman—I wish I
were.

There is this further evil that church architects, forced to be Gothic by the clergy and
their congregations, are cut off from real
religious expression by sham religious expression. So, finally, I would insist that the prob-

lem of the Society for the Protection of Ancient Buildings is not merely restoration, but the whole problem of church architecture. This Society is not merely an Antiquarian Society trying to preserve things as if they were in a museum; its cause is the cause of all true architecture. This Society wishes to preserve things precisely because it does not want anybody to imitate them. It would preserve them as examples, but as examples which are not to be imitated because they themselves did not imitate anything. If you can grasp the fact that Gothic is original architecture in which men were really expressing themselves, and really solving the structural problems of their time, that it has the thrill in it of people making discoveries, a thrill which nobody can imitate, then you will not try to imitate it— and then you will wish to protect an ancient building because, although there are great works of art all through the ages, you can never have precisely that one again. You can never recover the particular state of feeling expressed in it. It is an unique creation once and for all. I take it that is the real principle of the Society; and for that reason the Society must advocate originality in architecture. And I think that, if once we grasp these principles, we shall see that we can have religious expression in architecture now only with austerity. I do not mean that austerity is necessary always ; but, if you have been a drunkard, moderate drinking is impossible and you must take the pledge. We have had so much clap-trap, so much insincerity, so much machine-made and imitative ornament, that for the time we have got to do without ornament altogether. Our case is like that of writers who fill their writing with " clichés," with dead metaphors which get in the way of what they want to say ; they must give up all metaphors and learn to express themselves in the simplest language. At present our architecture is full of dead metaphors ; and it must be purged of them. We must aim only at the sense of things in our building. Then, when by that process we have recovered our reason and logic, the natural inclination for ornament will return and find genuine expression. But for the time we suffer from dipsomania and must take the pledge. By austerity we shall be forced to true invention ; but now, unfortunately, our lack of true invention is concealed from us by imitation, so that we do not feel the want ; we do not feel the urgent desire for real invention that we ought to feel. We are in the position of people who have no balance at the bank but keep on drawing cheques ; and the cheques are honoured. If the cheques were dishonoured, then we should see that we must get a balance at all costs. So now we should refuse to draw on the past. We have no balance, no capital ; we have to make a capital. We must be honest and face our destitution ; then gradually we shall get a balance.

VI

The Problem of Evil ◠　　◠　　◠

WE speak of the Problem of Evil, but not
of the Problem of Good ; which means
that the existence of evil surprises us,
and we never grow used to it. We appear to
be born with the expectation of a universe in
which things will be as we wish them to be, and
we find ourselves in one where things are sometimes as we wish them to be and sometimes
not. In this universe there is life, which
implies conditions favourable to life ; and there
is also death, which implies conditions un-
favourable to life. But one of the necessary
conditions favourable to life is in life itself,
namely the desire and the effort to persist. To
that desire, to that effort, the problem of evil
is practical, it is the problem of avoiding
death ; and this existed for living creatures
ages before men began to ask why there is evil
or death in the universe. So the theoretical
or philosophical problem has grown out of the
practical problem ; and there remains always
some of the urgency of the practical problem in

the theoretical. It is life itself, and the desire and effort of life to persist, that makes us ask why there is in the universe a something hostile to life ; life itself makes us see the universe in terms of its friendship or hostility to life and gives us our passionate desire to prove that, finally, the universe is friendly to life ; for life itself is lessened by its own fears of a hostile universe.

Yet good and evil do not present themselves to living creatures as life and death, but rather as pleasure and pain. Death is always in the future for all things that are living ; but pain is often in the present, and it is not merely the threat of death but something immediately evil in itself. Without pain, death would not be an evil in itself ; it would be an evil only in so far as it put an end to the pleasures of life ; and so, if we call it an evil in itself, we imply that the pleasures of life exceed its pains and that life, in the main, is good. But this implication, which is in our avoidance of even painless death, is not theory or philosophy so much as the effort of life to persist ; and pain itself, the very type of all evil, is part of that effort ; for it is a warning of something dangerous to life given by life to itself. It has its uses to life, even if it makes life intolerable ; for without it we should never learn to avoid a thousand dangers. The burnt child, for instance, would not dread the fire, but might, for lack of the warning of pain, suffer a painless extinction by burning.

Yet this value of pain to life does not make pain any more pleasant to the animal, nor does it solve the problem of evil for man. What he desires is not merely life but a life worth living, that is to say a life of pleasure rather than of pain. In fact, the worst nightmare he has ever conceived, and the extremity of evil to him, is a life of eternal pain. Besides, pain has not always value ; it persists when warnings are no longer of any use, in the vain effort of life itself to persist when death is certain. And so the problem of evil is not really the problem of death, but rather the problem, why there should be this blind effort of life to persist through pains that greatly exceed pleasures, and in spite, even, of the desire of the living creature to die. There seems to be an indifference in life itself to the feelings of the living creature ; a pitiless distinction between life and the living creature, as if we were possessed by a force not ourselves, although we cannot exist without it, which will torture us so that it may persist in us as long as possible. Why this should be, is the problem of evil in its most naked form ; why should there be a universe of such a nature that life itself may persist in the living creature only by torturing it, and often by vainly torturing it ? For the end of its effort to persist is death.

Here, of course, by isolating the problem of evil, I have exaggerated evil. Life does not usually persist by means of torture to the living creature and, in any case, cannot so persist for very long. It may be that, as a rule the pleasures of life exceed its pains ; but the problem of evil remains for us, no matter how much we may be enjoying ourselves, in the possibility of these pains for ourselves, in their existence for others. Say, if you will, that the worst tortures of an individual have their value to the human race in that the human race is, by the spectacle of them, incited to a sharper struggle with pain and death ; but still you are making that distinction between life and the particular living creature which is the very essence of the problem of evil. And still the question remains, Why should there be this distinction ; why should life persist and strengthen and intensify itself thus through the pains of the individual ?

Is not this very distinction which you make between life and the individual only an effort to justify evil ? You know nothing of life except in living creatures ; and in itself it is good or evil only as it is good or evil to them. The problem of evil would not be solved if we knew that all living creatures at some future

The Problem of Evil

time would live an eternal life of perfect joy, and that our pains were a means for the achievement of that millennium; for there would still remain the problem, Why should the millennium be achieved by that means?

And now it is clear that the problem of evil, as soon as it passes from the practical to the theoretical, becomes a moral problem. The desire of the animal, absorbed in the practical problem, is to avoid pain and enjoy pleasure, and this desire persists in man; but, when man turns to the theoretical problem, he is possessed by another desire, namely to convince himself that the conscience of man is, in some way, shared by the universe, that it is neither hostile nor indifferent to the aims of that conscience, and that man's conscience is valued by him because it is not only his own but shared by him with something higher, or, to use theological language, that it is transcendent as well as immanent.

I am here concerned merely with the desire, not with the question whether it is based on fact and can be gratified. Behind every effort of man there is a desire of some kind; and we must know what the desire is if we would understand the effort. Much effort has been spent, whether vainly or not, upon the problem of evil; and, if we would know clearly what the problem is, we must know what is the desire that makes men attempt to solve it. They may sometimes have persuaded themselves that they were trying to solve it for the sake of solving it; but, in that case, being unaware of their suppressed desire, they were not aware of the nature of the problem which that desire had set them. Much philosophy is confused by unacknowledged desire; the philosopher thinks that the wish to reach a certain conclusion would be unphilosophic in him; he therefore remains unaware of it and yet it guides him, like a natural force, to that conclusion. His problem really is to reach that conclusion by a process that will convince his reason; and he would be more of a philosopher if he acknowledged the fact, if he saw that his aim was to convince his reason and not merely to exercise it.

If we could prove that the conscience of man is peculiar to man and not shared, in any way, by the universe, we should not have solved the problem of evil to our own satisfaction; we should only have discovered certain facts which made that problem insoluble, for the desire behind the problem would remain unsatisfied. Let us then acknowledge the desire, so that we may understand the nature of the problem.

It may be that, as soon as we do acknowledge the desire, we shall cease to concern ourselves

The Problem of Evil

with the problem. Good and evil alike, we may say, are good and evil only to us. It is vain to demand that they shall also be good and evil to that abstraction which we call the universe. All living things are subject to pleasure and pain, the simplest forms of good and evil, and that is all we know about it. Our conscience, so far as we can see, exists only in us. It has increased, intensified and, to some extent, changed good and evil for us, so that they are not merely pleasure or pain as they are for animals. Let us then trust to this conscience in ourselves without trying to see it anywhere else. Let the problem, however much it may change with our ideas of good and evil, still remain a practical problem for us, namely to seek good and avoid evil.

Unfortunately our very ideas of good and evil have become such that the theoretical problem is for us also a practical problem. Just as good and evil no longer remain merely pleasure and pain to us, so we are not content with any view of life which makes it the pursuit of pleasure or the avoidance of pain. There is for us evil in the very notion of an indifferent universe; it is something that we desire to escape from; and this desire, though it expresses itself in thought, is just as practical as all other desires. It has an aim which, though it can be achieved by thought not action, is yet a practical aim. The desire is a fact from which we cannot escape; and the obstacles to it are also facts. The problem is to convince the reason that what we wish to believe is true; and that problem is not solved by declaring it insoluble. It remains, as the desire remains, and, if we would get rid of it, we must get rid of the desire. But we can get rid of the desire only by convincing ourselves, not that it is vain—for that will never remove it, since as long as we desire we shall refuse to believe that the desire is vain—but by convincing ourselves that the desire is not one of our deepest and most permanent desires, that it is contrary to the values which are caused by our deepest and most permanent desires.

But these values are precisely for a universal conscience, a harmony of all things, both in ideas of good and evil and in the pursuit of good and avoidance of evil. In fact our very ideas of good and evil are themselves made by this desire for a universal harmony. Rightly or wrongly we are committed, not only in theory but in practice, not only to a dream, but to an effort, to achieve a universal harmony. Our ideas of good and evil may differ, but in so far as they differ we believe that there is error in them; and our conduct may lead to conflict but, in so far as it does,

The Problem of Evil

we believe that there is sin in it. We may despair of a millennium, but still we value our desire for it above all things. We may not believe that the lion will ever lie down with the lamb, but we cannot persuade ourselves, cannot even try to persuade ourselves, that the desire expressed in those words is a morally wrong desire. In the world as we know it, living things necessarily prey on each other; we may not have a sense of sin in that we ourselves prey on other living creatures; but we do desire a world in which we shall not prey on them; and that desire is one we cannot but value. Further, any conception we may have of perfect happiness would mean a happiness shared by all living things and consisting in a harmony alike of desire and accomplishment. The greatest happiness of which we are capable consists in some realization, however imperfect, of this harmony. It comes to us sometimes in art or worship, and then we call it heaven. It is something very different from conceptions of happiness possible to an animal, something much later in the development of the mind; but we value the mind because it is capable of that conception, and development means advance to us because it has, however dimly, reached that conception. Evil itself becomes to us more and more clearly all that, in ourselves and outside ourselves, frustrates our desire for the harmony which alone can be happiness.

Therefore it is impossible that we should get rid of the desire to convince ourselves that the universe is not indifferent to our ideas of good and evil, since we cannot desire to get rid of that desire. A universe so indifferent to us would be evil to us, would make us despair if we were convinced of it. Yet there are signs of that indifference everywhere. So our problem, practical as well as theoretical, is to convince our reason, that the universe is not indifferent; and that *is* the problem of evil, itself both theoretical and practical.

If it be said that this is not a philosophical problem at all since it is practical—that, if we try to convince our reason of the truth of that which we desire to be true, we are not engaged in a rational process—I would answer, that in that case we can never, except perhaps in pure mathematics, be engaged in a rational process. For all our activities are efforts to accomplish some desire. Further, what is really unphilosophical is to ignore the desire and to pretend that the result is reached without regard to any desire; and this, I think, is a game philosophers are always playing, through a false analogy between science and philosophy. There is a psychological difference between the two that must not be ignored. Science may

The Problem of Evil

have an immediate practical aim, as, in medicine, the aim of dealing with certain physical facts so as to subject them to the will of man. So that that aim may be accomplished, it is necessary to discover the exact nature of the facts, and the desire is to discover their exact nature so that the other desire to master them may be satisfied. There is also science which has no immediate practical aim, such as the science of Astronomy. But behind this also there is some desire, which it is difficult to discover precisely. It is not a desire for knowledge for its own sake, because there is some principle in it which determines the relative importance of different kinds of knowledge. It may be ultimately the desire for mastery, or for a feeling of mastery that is given by knowledge, or it may be the philosophic desire for the discovery of a harmony. In any case the astronomer has the right to ignore his desire because he cannot be sure what it is ; while the doctor is in no danger of ignoring his desire because he knows clearly what it is and it conditions his whole activity. But the philosopher has no right to ignore his desire, if it is there and if it really conditions his activity. If evil is a problem to him, because of his desire to explain it, and if it is impossible for him and for all men to rid themselves of this desire, then let him acknowledge the fact to himself; let him state it to others. There is nothing wrong in the desire, unless it causes him to ignore or pervert facts; but it is more likely to do that if unacknowledged and unconscious than if conscious and acknowledged. If he sees and says that the problem for him is to reconcile the facts with his desire, then he will see also that it is no solution of that problem to ignore or pervert facts. His desire is, not to do that but, given the facts, to convince his reason of what he wishes to believe. The facts are facts, reason is impartial; his desire cannot be achieved by juggling with either.

So much then for the problem of evil. I will end with a recapitulation.

There are two problems of evil, a practical and a theoretical, but the theoretical problem has also the practical persisting in it. The practical problem is to avoid or remove evil. The theoretical is to find an explanation of the existence of evil which will allow us to believe well of the universe, to believe that in some way it shares the conscience of man. This is also practical, because a universe which does not share our conscience is itself evil to us, and so, in idea, one of the evils we wish to remove.

We shall not remove it by juggling; for in

The Problem of Evil

the long run such juggling will help to convince us, not only that the universe is evil, but that it has a peculiarly malignant power of deceiving us, and that we are evil because we do incessantly deceive ourselves. Nothing produces the worst of mental nightmares, the nightmare of universal illusion, so much as dishonest thinking about evil. There is indeed a whole doctrine of universal illusion, a whole psychology and even philosophy of it, which is a reaction from dishonest thinking about evil. But just as sentimentality comes into philosophy and frustrates it, so also in reply satire comes into it and equally frustrates it. Just as there is a blind desire to think well of the universe and ourselves at all costs, so this same desire frustrated turns into its contrary, a desire to think ill of both at all costs. If there is a general tendency to sacrifice truth to desire, it provokes a general tendency to believe that truth cannot be discovered. But this latter cuts its own throat, since if truth cannot be discovered, if we are necessarily subject to illusion about all our own mental operations, then those operations have no validity, even when they prove that we are necessarily subject to illusion. We are, in fact, as the lawyers say " estopped " from believing any theory that metaphysically discredits the human mind, since such a theory makes all belief impossible. But, if the human mind is not discredited, then its desires are facts of the universe which our philosophy must take into account.

VII

Creative Religion ～ ～ ～

THE MODERN SENSE OF VALUES

THE philosophy of Herbert Spencer has suddenly lost all its influence. We do not attack it; we ignore it. It has gone out of fashion. It does not answer, it does not even ask, the questions we ask. In the completeness of our reaction we may not be just to it; but what is the reason of that reaction? It is not merely that we are tired of Spencer, that we look for something newer, but that in all his works there is one great assumption which we instinctively deny. He is ready, and even anxious, to believe something that we refuse to believe; and all the implications of his thought are rejected by us.

The assumption is that all man's deepest values are imposed upon him by external circumstances; and that, if those circumstances could be changed, his values would change with them. Man, in his thoughts and emotions and conscience, is entirely moulded by his surroundings, which means his material surroundings;

and that reality which he is so intensely aware
of within himself is less real than the reality
outside himself of which his senses make him
aware. Spencer in fact affirms, or rather implies as if it needed no affirmation, that this
external reality is the only reality, and that
our values are a mere comment upon it, a
theorizing about it which has become habitual
and instinctive. For him the emotional part
of those values, the passion which we have for
truth, beauty and righteousness, is an illusion,
even if a useful illusion. We should lose that
passion with fuller knowledge, and should become completely reasonable beings, adapting
ourselves perfectly and consciously to the
business of continuing to live, which is the
only real business we have.

It would be easy to find passages in Spencer
inconsistent with this assumption, for all philosophers are inconsistent, but the assumption is
constant, and against it we rebel. For in less
than a generation a change has come over our
thought, a change so great that we have not
yet succeeded in expressing it, and are scarcely
aware how great it is. But, when people talk
of the revival of religion, they mean this
change, if they mean anything at all ; we no
longer believe that our values are imposed on
us by our external circumstances, or that the
emotional force in those values, the passion for

truth, beauty and righteousness, is merely a useful illusion.   Rather we seek for an explanation of the nature of the universe in those values.   They are to us more real than external reality.   We believe that we ourselves, that is, our thoughts, our emotions, our conscience, are more real than our material surroundings, and that we are not passive material moulded by those surroundings, but active beings with an activity which we call spiritual.

This belief, which is gaining everywhere, even in people who are hardly conscious of it, is very old, but it is finding for itself new expression and a new confidence because of the modern ordeals through which it has passed. It has, in fact, passed through the ordeal of Herbert Spencer's philosophy and through the whole evolutionary theory upon which that philosophy is based ; and now it is beginning to react on the evolutionary theory itself. There is a refusal to accept any theory which regards man, or indeed any living creature, as purely passive material, and an attempt to find in life itself the power of its own evolution, the scent for its own future.   And in man, the highest form of life known to us, we find that scent in our own values.   They, rather than the play of circumstances, are the force that works changes in us.   It is our passion for something not ourselves, not our desire to be ourselves as long as possible, which makes us ourselves and gives us the very test of what we call progress.

All the implications of this belief have not been stated; it has logical consequences of which we are not yet fully aware; but it is certainly true that it makes for a revival of religion. For what is religion but an affirmation of absolute values? What is the belief in God but a belief in a Person of absolute value? And the belief in God, so far as it is a religious belief at all and not a mere desire for help or comfort, is produced by the sense of absolute values, the sense that they are not for mere abstractions but for a single and personal reality. There is still a surviving prejudice against this belief in God as something unscientific and superstitious; and it remains to be proved that it is neither— that it is the logical and inevitable result of our belief in our own values, and, more than that, the result of those values when they are obeyed by the whole will and the whole mind. That, as we say, remains to be proved, but the intellect of the world is now turning towards the proof of it. It is no longer possessed by the superstition that the belief in God must be superstitious. We have entered upon a new period of creative religion, all the more creative because it is not yet consciously religious. And we reject the philosophy of Spencer because there is no hint or promise or hope of religion to be found in it.

FAITH AND REASON

The most hopeful fact about religion now is the flow of intelligence into it. A generation ago intelligence, when it concerned itself with religion, usually took the form either of learning or of apology. That is to say, it was occupied rather with the past than with the present, and there always seemed to be some unreality in its activities. It assumed that its task was only to preserve; it commented and explained; it did not try to create. In the last century the religious controversies were between those who would preserve all the assertions of the past and those who, whether within the Church or outside it, would deny some of them. Both took it for granted that the faith was complete; the only question was whether or not it had gone too far and asserted too much.

Now the question is rather whether we cannot find a better expression for the faith, and this question is one with which the intellect can concern itself without any sense of unreality. A dogma is no longer something to be merely attacked or defended; it is seen to be the form given in the past to a certain belief, and a form which therefore is not necessarily final or perfect. It may be improved or changed altogether without changing the belief which it expresses, and the intellectual effort now is to discover the precise nature of that belief. Therefore it is no longer an effort of attack or defence, but rather one of discovery; and it implies co-operation rather than controversy.

Hence the great desire felt by all religious people for unity. They desire it because they feel that the old differences no longer have any reality. They are not attacking or defending; rather they are, like men of science, all discovering and able to help each other in the task of discovery. What we ask now is, What do we really believe? And our aim is to know what we do believe and to express our belief in our own terms. Further, we have the conviction that, if only we can find that expression, we shall find also that there is little difference in our beliefs. It is the more or less obsolete expressions of the past that make the differences seem much greater than they are. And so, among religious people, the desire to make proselytes has almost ceased: for they see that there is something unreal in the effort to convince people that some one past expression of belief is better than another, when what is needed is a present expression convincing in its own truth and beauty. Religion in this

Creative Religion

respect is very like art. If it is to live and not to be a matter only for specialists and antiquaries, it must find its own living expression in every age. Michelangelo may be the greatest artist that ever lived ; but, if we really care for art, we cannot live on his works ; we want painting and sculpture of our own time to express ourselves, and the production of them is the natural expression of our own love of art. But in the matter of religion we are all artists, and must all produce our own natural expression of our beliefs, which will necessarily differ from the expressions of the past if they are our own and sincere.

So long as the intelligence was concerned merely with attacking or defending dogmas this was not understood ; and it was supposed that religion itself must be destroyed or changed with any change in its expression. This idea prevailed because religion was thought of as something handed down from the past, something which the present could only preserve or destroy. Now we think of it as something which springs up fresh in the hearts of men, as a living fact like art, and one which no change of expression can destroy. We have in fact a much greater faith in it, and in the nature of man. We believe that truth is born in men's minds as well as error ; that it is something which man recognizes, not something which he has to accept in mere blind obedience. And for this truth, since it is his, he must find his own expression. The old notion was that men would naturally believe any folly and wickedness about the universe; and that they could be preserved from these only by precise statements of the truth, which must be always the same, and which they must accept if they were not to yield to the naughtiness of their own hearts. This notion was not faith but unfaith; the religious faith is that men have a desire for the truth and a power of recognizing it, and of giving their own expression to it; and further that, so far as they are filled with a sincere desire for it they will attain to it, and therefore to the same belief.

What we need, therefore, is not blind obedience, but sincerity of desire; and in the results of that desire, wherever it exists, we must have faith. Also sincerity of desire is encouraged in men by the free play of the intelligence. So long as they are told not to seek, but to obey, the truth, presented to them as something discovered once and for all in the past, does not seem to them worth having. They must have faith in their own power of recognizing it if they are to desire it passionately. That is how science has flourished in our time; it has been a quest of the truth, impassioned by the faith that it can be recognized when seen, and freed from the burden of authority. Only so will religion flourish and engage the best intellect of our time. That intellect is already turning to it of its own accord, and it must be welcomed, not rebuffed, by the Church. For, if it is rebuffed, it will still concern itself with religion and the Church will be to it merely an academic institution that does not understand its own business. It needs to be clearly understood that the very expression of religious belief is the task not only of the clergy, but of all men ; and that those who seek to find a new expression for it are not the enemies either of the Church or of religion.

The Modern Distrust of Religion

Many people of all classes have now a deep distrust of all religion, as if it must imply some kind of dishonesty, moral or intellectual, as if there must be some motive other than a desire for the truth in all religious belief. A clergyman believes, to put it coarsely, because he would lose his living if he ceased to do so ; a layman, because he gets some kind of comfort from his beliefs.

This suspicion is encouraged by much vague talk about religion ; and we are asked to compare it with the precise statements of men of science, who never assert anything that they cannot prove. The comparison is not quite fair, because of the difference in the subject matter ; one might as well be suspicious of all morality because there is much vague talk about it. Certainly there is some motive other than the desire for truth in all religious belief ; but so there is in all moral belief. In both cases there is the will to believe. But the most rigid agnostic can profess his faith in the moral law without being accused of dishonesty. Often, indeed, agnostics insist on their faith in the moral law as something superior to all religion ; always they insist on their passion for truth at all costs. But the basis of their faith and their passion is the will to believe. Their very contempt for those who believe what makes them comfortable is based on a pure assumption that men ought to believe what is true rather than what makes them comfortable. They may think that, in the long run, to believe for the sake of comfort leads to disaster, that it is ruinous to a whole society if not to an individual. But they must know that it is possible for an individual to believe for the sake of comfort and to remain comfortable all his life ; and why should the individual care about the fate of society ? Why, except on certain assumptions which are the result of the will to believe just as much as any religious assumptions ?

The agnostic may say that these assumptions

are natural to him, that he has a passion for the truth, which he must gratify as if it were an appetite ; but in that case, why should he express moral contempt of those who are without it ? That contempt in him must be inconsistent with his own passion for the truth ; for the truth to the complete agnostic is that he has no right to think his own values higher than anyone else's. There are no higher or lower values ; there are merely values.

But this no one, not even Nietzsche, has ever believed. It was his doctrine that all beliefs are the result of the will to power ; and yet he constantly expressed moral indignation against those who hid truth from themselves. He could not attain to the ultimate scepticism about the value of truth ; he had his morality, like every one else ; and, like all the sceptics, he had that will to believe in matters of morality which is thought to be so dishonest in matters of religion.

And yet what is religion in its essence but a more passionate and logical expression of the moral faith ? There are certain abstractions which the moralist worships—goodness, truth, beauty—and to which he says we must sacrifice everything ; but they remain for him abstractions, and therefore they have for him, in theory at least, no real existence. He is content that they should be only names to him—perhaps he worships only one of them, truth, and deduces the value of the others from that; he will not formulate any creed about them; he will not build a temple to them. But still he worships them, and from that worship derives all his sense of purpose in life, all his judgments, all his approved will. It is in their defence that he will sacrifice his life now; and by that alone we know that they are not really names to him but something more, however firmly he may refuse to confess it.

But the religious man is conscious of the fact that these things are not merely abstractions or names to him, and he expresses that fact in his faith. Truth, righteousness and beauty have a reality for him too intense to be expressed in any abstract words and too completely one to be expressed separately. His value for them is not three values, but one value; and the more he is aware that it is one value the more he sees that it is a value for a person and not for an abstraction. Hence the belief in God, which is the result of passionate values fused into one value, a result which happens to certain people, at least, just as naturally as the simple value for truth happens to others. So those who are joyfully possessed by the value for truth have no right to sneer at the religious mind or to accuse it of any kind of dishonesty.

Creative Religion

It is true that all seeming religion has not been the result of this passion for truth, beauty and righteousness. But we have no right to judge any activity of the mind of man by its failures and perversions. If religion has some disreputable ancestors, so has science. There is imperfection in both, and neither has the right to throw stones because of it. The modern scientific distrust of religion is no more scientific than the old religious distrust of science was religious.

What is Religion ?

I have been asked to define what we mean by religion; and some of those who ask seem to think that we have no right to use the word at all unless we can instantly define it in a sentence. But many things which exist are not easy to define. There is art, for instance, which people have been trying to define for a century or more; and there is life itself. It exists and we have a right to talk about it; but who can define it ? Only those who are determined to express some theory of their own in their definition.

Religion is almost as difficult to define as life, because, like art, it springs out of the whole life of man; and our very conception of religion must depend upon our conception of the life of man. There is a religious conception of life—

namely, that it has a purpose and is life because it has this purpose. According to that conception, man can be explained only in terms of what he is trying to become and not in terms of his origins. Religion is his effort to make this purpose clearer to himself; and at the same time to fulfil it more consciously. It is thought and feeling and conduct; all aiming at the expression and at the fulfilment of this purpose; and the purpose is what gives unity to all its manifestations. According to this view religion itself, like life, can be explained only in terms of what it is trying to become; hence the difficulty of defining it. We cannot be content to define it merely by the observation of past or present examples, because in them there is only the effort to be religion, as in man himself there is the effort to be something more than he is. As he follows the scent of his own future, so religion follows the scent of its own future. There never yet has been any pure religion, as there never has been any pure art or pure humanity. And that is the reason why we cannot define any one of these so as to satisfy ourselves or anyone else.

Of course, those who do not hold the religious view of life may frame hostile definitions of religion to express their own dislike of it. They may define it as the belief in that which is not true. But any definition of religion as merely belief is inadequate, and is based upon the observation of past or present examples of religion by those who do not believe in them. To those who do fully believe a religion, it is always more than belief; it is always works, as well as faith; and it is a co-operation of both in the effort to attain to a state of being in which they shall act and react on each other in perfect harmony. In the past many religions have failed to be religious because they have consisted of faith without works, or of faith which forced men into actions against their own conscience; and the mind of man always tends thus to divorce faith from works and to pervert faith, and religion itself, by this divorce. There is life and growth in religion only when faith and works have an equal part in it, when each enriches and controls the other. Faith directs conduct, and conduct develops and clarifies faith, which, being thus developed and clarified, does in its turn give a yet more precise direction to conduct.

This is the doctrine of Christianity; and this very doctrine implies that Christianity is not a static faith, that it is perverted from its true nature the moment it becomes static. It is a faith that must live in works, must be always directed and enriched by works, or it ceases to be the Christian faith. Hence it cannot be preserved from age to age unless it grows from

age to age. To hand it down is not enough ;
it may be a dead thing that is handed down.
For its very creed is in works, as well as in
faith. It is a dogma of Christianity that it
cannot be believed except by those who practise it ; hence every failure in practice produces
a failure or a perversion of belief, and the history of Christianity is full of these failures and
perversions. But it remains always something
to be discovered by man, as the purpose of his
life remains to be discovered, more and more
fully and clearly by the co-operation of faith
and works.

It may be denied that any advance has ever
been made in the discovery of either. There
are some to whom Christianity is a static
truth ; others to whom it is a static lie. They
would both define religion as merely faith,
whether in what is true or in what is untrue ;
and to them, therefore, definition would be
easy. But it is not easy to those who hold the
religious view of life, because for them religion
is the effort of man to make the purpose of his
life clearer to himself and to fulfil that purpose ;
it is religion because it is not merely thought
or conduct or feeling, but a united effort of all
three, the only effort of man in which all three
have an equal part and the same ultimate
object. As to that ultimate object, it cannot
be defined, for it is the very purpose of religion

to discover it. Only those who hold the religious view of life believe that men can, by the co-operation of faith and works, come nearer and nearer to the discovery of it. Their faith is in works, in the power of conduct, directed by faith, to discover truths which cannot be discovered by the pure intelligence. That is the point at which they differ from the agnostic, although he, too, will usually admit that moral truths can be understood only by those who act on them. But he is content to act upon moral truths without trying to state them; whereas the religious effort is also to state them with all their implications, and, by the statement of them, to make the connexion between faith and works always closer.

Reality and Christianity

People are always saying now that the religion preached by the Church of England is unreal. Often they do not know what they mean when they say this. Their discontent is vague, and vaguely expressed. But they do mean something. What is it? It is, we think, that the theology of the Church has shrunk into a series of statements about supernatural history which have no clear connexion with the life of man, and that there is a barren conflict within the Church about these statements, a conflict which itself has no connexion with the life of man, but is a mere game for specialists.

If Christianity still exists, if it is not merely a number of survivals becoming more and more separate from each other, it is a belief about the nature of the universe which should have a universal influence on the conduct of those who hold it, which should give passion to their thought and joy to their actions. It cannot be merely practical morality nor a system of ethics. If it still has a right to call itself a religion, if it keeps its old unity, its old claim to supremacy over the whole mind of man, it must be able to convince men that they are of a certain nature and part of a universe of a certain nature ; and it must be able to make its statements about the nature of man and of the universe spontaneously and naturally in terms of modern thought, just as Christ and St. Paul spoke spontaneously and naturally in terms of the thought of their time.

Certainly the Church has not done this yet ; and those who accuse it of unreality mean perhaps that the Church could not do it ; that it clings to old statements because it does not know clearly what Christianity would be in terms of modern thought, because it wishes to preserve Christianity with the authority of the past, and fears that it cannot live by its own truth. But those who believe that it can live by its own truth will wish for a statement of that truth as it would naturally present itself to men now. The real conflict for them is not between those who believe in the Virgin Birth and those who do not, between those who would preserve and those who would destroy the past authority of Christianity; but between those for whom it is a new truth confirmed and enriched by their own experience, and those for whom it is mischievous and sentimental nonsense refuted by all the facts of the modern world.

To Nietzsche, for instance, it was mischievous and sentimental nonsense, because he believed that the will to power was the ultimate fact in human nature and that the nature of the universe was in accordance with that fact. So, when Christ tells us, as he does, to put off our will to power, he tells us to do what we cannot do and what therefore it is wrong to attempt. The question, the real question, for men now is whether Christ or Nietzsche is right; and that will not be settled by appeal to the authority of Christ; rather the authority of Christ will depend upon the answer that is given by men out of their own experience.

But Christianity tells us that we cannot give the right answer merely by means of our observation of the natural order of things. It tells us that there is, as a matter of fact, another

87

order transcending the natural order which we cannot be aware of unless we ourselves transcend it by putting off our will to power, by seeing all men and things, not as they are of use to us, but as they have virtue or beauty in themselves. It tells us that, if we do this, we shall be aware of a reality compared with which the will to power and the struggle for life are unreal. Now the question whether this is true or not is a real question of immediate moment to all men, and one which they can answer by means of actual experiment. Upon the answer we make to it will depend our theory of the State and all our practical politics. And there is another assertion of Christianity closely connected with it and of equal moment. It is that the ultimate reality of the universe is not a process, such as the struggle for life, but a person, God. This we cannot prove with any certainty out of our own experience. But, if we believe it, we shall value all persons, that is to say all men, more than any process. The test for us of our conduct will be, not whether we are acting in accordance with any process which we believe to be supreme, but whether we are showing reverence and love for any particular person with whom we have to do ; and we shall refuse to sacrifice any particular person, no matter how mean or weak, to any process whatsoever.

Creative Religion

Christianity says that all men are the children of God; if these words mean anything they mean that all men are alike in their nobler faculties, alike in kind if not in degree; and that out of this likeness a fellowship can be attained to, which is not a mere association for the better waging of the struggle for life, but is itself a transcendence of that struggle. If the Church is anything, it is, or tries to be, such a fellowship; if the nation is to rise above mere nationalism, it also must become such a fellowship; if the world is not for ever to be the cockpit it now is, it also must become such a fellowship. So long as we conceive of the universe as a cockpit we shall make the world one; and at present it is quite possible for men who call themselves Christians to conceive of the universe as a cockpit, and to believe that they have reconciled science and Christianity by doing so. That is why men say that the teaching of the Church is unreal. It does not control the real thought of its members. They can think that they believe its creed and yet remain heretics about the nature of the universe. No doubt that is their stupidity; but it is this stupidity, this kind of profound and unconscious heresy, that the Church must deal with by a new statement of the truths of Christianity. Above all, it must prove that it is a fellowship, not in the struggle for life nor in

7   89

the struggle for salvation, but because it asserts that all men in their nobler faculties are alike, and that they will attain to the fellowship of the world only by trust in these nobler faculties.

MECHANICAL RELIGION

Every one knows that there are mechanical practices in our religion and that it is easy to fall into them: though they are never quite so much systematized as the Prayer Wheels of Tibet, those symbols of all mechanical religion about which we used often to be told in sermons. But it is not so commonly known that there are also mechanical theories of religion, into which it is very easy to fall, and to think them the most orthodox certainty. We are accustomed to think of mechanical theories of the universe as anti-religious. They postulate no god, but a mechanical process to which man is utterly subject, of which he is a part.

But these theories are only the conscious acceptance of an inveterate tendency in the mind of man, a tendency which existed long before man had any machinery and which is always creeping into all his thought and suppressing all his more generous emotions. True religion protests against this tendency; it insists that person, in God and in man, is more real than any process; that we must always value person, and every person, above process,

90

and that we only attain to wisdom when we see person as the reality and process merely as a comment of our own minds. But there is always a false religion in which the sense of process prevails again over the sense of person, so that salvation itself is thought of as a process to which person is utterly subject and which can be achieved only by the utter submission of person to its mechansm.

This mechanical religion, as we have said, always sees itself as the most perfect ortho- doxy. There is one exact method of achiev- ing salvation and no other ; and this has been ordained by God. Men have no need to think about it or to consider it in the light of them- selves, of their own values. To do that is dangerous ; it is to meddle with the machinery. With regard to salvation all men are the same, merely rough material to be put through the machine ; and they will go through it easiest and quickest if they are quite passive under it. For the mechanically religious mind all the sacraments are merely a process and no one can be saved except by undergoing them. Peni- tence itself is a process to which all must submit in the same way. We have read, for instance, a tract lately, in which it was said that, since Christ had given the power of absolution to the priest, it was surely safest to seek absolu- tion in that manner, since in no other way could one be sure of getting it. That word *safest* betrays the mechanical mind ; for in real religion there is no question of safety. A man repents, not because he wishes to subject himself to a mechanical process of salvation, but because he knows that his sin cuts him off from God and man. It is man the person, and God the Person, that affects his mind. One cannot repent as one would take medicine, merely to get rid of a discomfort. One can subject oneself to a mechanical process for that purpose, but that is not repentance.

No doubt many who repent find that they do so best by confessing and obtaining absolution ; it is a method which reminds them that they are sinners. But, if repentance is their aim, they do not practise the method for the sake of safety. Nor do they believe that it is the only method ; to do that is to degrade it at once into a mechanical process. It may be the best for A but not for B ; and A should be content with the fact that he finds it best for himself. The present deep prejudice against orthodox religion is not all mere bigotry ; it is partly itself religious and a protest against mechanical orthodoxy, against the notion that anybody can lay claim to the one and only method of salvation. There may be a best method ; but that cannot be the best for which such claims are made. The right of private judgment is not insisted upon out of pure wilfulness ; nor does it mean that any one man's judgment is necessarily as good as another's. It is a proclamation of the supremacy of person, and of every person, over process. A man can know for himself whether he needs to repent and also whether he does repent ; and he can know this without submitting to any external process. The more religious he is the less likely he is to suppose that God has imposed any one infallible process on mankind as a means to salvation. With all the help offered by the Churches, he still has to find his own way to God, and to attain to his own knowledge of Him. For God is a Person, that is the knowledge to which he attains ; and for God each man must be a person too, and not merely raw material to be subjected to a process of salvation.

It is well to speak plainly on this matter ; because the Church of England now is honestly anxious to know why so many people, in their nature religious, are indifferent to her. It is because they find so much that is mechanical in her teaching, and especially in the teaching of those who think themselves most orthodox. There is, of course, no need for that teaching to be mechanical ; it becomes mechanical only in the hands of those who do not understand its true meaning, and especially of those who insist that they alone have the right method. Such a recommendation is no recommendation to the really religious mind of to-day. What we seek is a method that shall live in the presentment of it, not one that dies on the hands of those who proclaim its infallibility. Anything that seems like magic now is dead to the religious mind ; what the Church needs is not a magic or a secret, but an art of life which will recommend itself by its own beauty, not by any proclamation of its claims.

VIII

An Unborn Catholicism 〄 〄

I

IN England, now, there is a great desire for
belief, satisfied by no existing church or
sect. There are still Rationalists, who
continue to prove that what is said in the Book
of Genesis about the creation of the world is
not true ; but they are a little negative sect by
themselves. Even the fun has died out of their
activities ; they have lost the joy of audacity.
We all know what they continue to prove ; and
our desire is to believe, not to disbelieve ; but
what ?

Many varieties of Christianity offer us belief ; but not one of them satisfies us. They
all have their convinced believers, but they do
not win the ablest, or the most naturally religious, among us. These do not reject Christianity ; they do not think that the Christian
effort of feeling, of thought, of conduct, which
has been maintained now for nearly two thousand years, has been futile or mistaken ; but
they are not content with any present state-

ment of the Christian faith. For these statements seem to them not to be serious enough ; they are like our modern Gothic churches, cumbered with the superfluous ornament of the past. What we need is not toy-shop Gothic, but a building of our own thought in which we can be at home. All existing forms of Christianity seem to wear fancy dress, and we are not comfortable in it. Yet we would not be cut off from the Christian tradition ; for we believe, far more than our fathers did, that the truth is hidden in it ; but it remains, for us, hidden.

The war has increased the desire for belief, not only in the weak, who seek consolation at all costs, but also in the strong, who see that science has not made us wise about the nature of the universe or our own nature. We know in our hearts that not only the Germans, but all of us, have been fools : we have believed something sillier than the silliest version of Christianity, namely, that mankind was advancing toward perfection by some mechanical process called evolution. This process we thought of as imposed on us by the nature of things ; all we had to do was not to impede it by faith in anything else. To the prosperous, it is always flattering to believe in the survival of the fittest : they survive, and so they are the fittest. If the master-fact of life is the struggle for life, they are succeeding in that struggle. The universe favours them, and they are content to be its puppets.

But now this struggle for life, as practised by the Germans, has turned into a struggle for death. They, most of all nations, were content to be the puppets of the universe; they made their will subject to the mechanism of things; and that mechanism has betrayed them. When we fought against them, we rebelled against the whole doctrine of the struggle for life; we affirmed the will of man, the will for righteousness; and, now that we have won, we are less than ever content to believe that we have survived because we are the fittest. For those whom we loved best have died for us; and we do not believe that they died because they were less fit than ourselves. They fought and died, not for us alone, nor for England alone, but for a universe of meaning; and what is the meaning of it?

Before the war it was a commonplace to sneer at the Christian doctrine of vicarious sacrifice, the doctrine of the Redemption. In our shallowness and comfort, we said that it was immoral; but now we know that the world is saved, and faith in the universe is preserved, by vicarious sacrifice. It is just because those who died for us, and for mankind, were better, not worse, than ourselves, that we begin to believe passionately in the meaning of the universe. For if it were a mechanism, whence comes that passion which sent the best joyfully to death ? " Yet a little while and the world seeth me no more ; but ye see me : because I live, ye shall live also." These words begin to have meaning for us ; not as spoken by one man, or God, to his disciples, but as spoken by all our dead to us. They live because they died for us ; and we live a life of meaning because of their sacrifice. Our logic of justice, by which a man pays for himself alone, is not the logic of God, as Christ said long ago. The universe is better than that : it is of such a nature that men can redeem each other and die for each other. So we begin again to believe that Christ did indeed die for us.

And we see that there is a surprising, unfathomed wisdom in the Christian faith. By ourselves we could never have discovered it, with all our knowledge of the mechanism of the stars. The way of our knowledge is not the way toward that wisdom. We made machines that would tear our best in pieces ; we devised new and more horrible crosses for them ; and on the cross they convince us that our power is only for destruction, and our wisdom foolishness. " Father, forgive them, for they know not what they do " ; that is the best that can be said for us, no less than for the Germans.

An Unborn Catholicism

And now we wish to know what we do. Nothing is stranger than the contrast between our disorder, impotence, and bewilderment in peace, and our power, resolution, and discipline in war. We made many mistakes; but our will was one and clear; and we accomplished it—I mean, not England alone, but all of us together. And there was this contrast, because in war we knew what we wished to do, and in peace we do not. Victory is a single aim, easily conceived and unanimously desired; but what is the aim of life? We have a thousand different answers; and many never even ask themselves the question. No nation, no parliament, asks it. No church answers it now, in terms that convince. And yet we believe that there is an answer that we can find; millions of us believe that Christ found it, if only we can understand His words and re-express them in our own. What we need is, to find the aim and to agree on it, all together; then we shall accomplish it, as we have accomplished victory, but with a greater joy and without the sacrifice of our best.

That, I believe, is the religious state of mind of the most naturally religious in my country. If it is less intense in America, it is because there you have suffered less, and because, perhaps, you have not been so foolish. Our old world has an intense life because of its enormities.

More Essays on Religion

In Europe, for many centuries, all the problems have forced themselves upon both thinkers and actors. We live crowded together among the glories and failures of the past ; we hate and love extremely ; there is instant retribution for our sins. It is but fifty years since we began to admire the success of Prussia, and to say in our hearts that her blood-and-iron creed was true and Christianity false. And now she has disproved it at a cost to herself, and to us, that you cannot by any effort of sympathy imagine. Or perhaps some of your old men, who remember your own war, can imagine it. But then your people was a simple people. It had not gone a-whoring after strange gods, nor had it said in its heart that there was no God. All the peoples of Europe have said that in their hearts, and now they know that in saying it they went a-whoring after the Prussian idol. Prussia is but the drunken helot for us all ; we too had our temples of Baal, our Ahabs and Jezebels ; but where is the Temple of the true God ?

II

There is the Roman Catholic Church. Its defect is that it belies its name and is no longer Catholic. Among the educated, only certain peculiarly minded people find themselves able to belong to it. It remains Catholic for the

An Unborn Catholicism

uneducated ; and that is why we are all drawn
toward it. For the Catholic element, the
Catholic desire in it, is of the greatest value ;
and we know that there is truth in it. But it
is a truth of feeling rather than of intellect.
The educated man must attain to that feeling
by a process which most educated men now
will not accept. They will not accept certain
postulates which seem to them arbitrary, chief
among them the doctrine of the infallibility of
the Pope. It does not matter that the Pope
in practice is seldom infallible ; that no one
knows quite certainly when he is infallible. It
is the doctrine that matters ; for it is the doctrine of authority. You must make a certain
surrender, not merely of yourself but of your
highest values, if you are to enter into that
Catholicity. You must become a pragmatist,
saying that that is truth which works ; and
that the Church, out of its immemorial experience, knows better than you do what does
work.

That is a surrender which only certain peculiarly minded people can make now. According to my observation, it is made usually by
those who are aware of some weakness in themselves which they despair of conquering. I
speak of converts, not of born Catholics. The
Catholic Church would say, of course, that we
all have some weakness which we cannot con-

quer without the help of God. That is true, and the Church is a kind, wise physician; but it offers you a perpetual rest-cure. It will never admit that you are well. The doctors themselves are valetudinarians; and they talk always the language of the sick-room. It is through your weakness that they draw you into their home, and it remains a home for the weak. Grant that they are often cured; but not by any means of a kind of hypnotism which must always continue. The Church, in fact, prefers hypnotism to psycho-analysis. And the wisest and bravest minds are turning to psycho-analysis, away from hypnotism. They would encourage the will rather than subdue it. They have trust in the mind of man, of every man, if only it can know itself. The Roman Church believes in a universal mind; but delegates it to a spiritual despot.

Next, there is the Church of England. It is both the glory and the shame of that Church that it does not really exist: it is always in process of becoming. The question now is, can it attain to existence? In the Church of England there are creeds; but there is no one, no body even, to interpret them. There is an organization; but no one, no body even, to govern it, except the State, which clearly is not the Church. The most real and impassioned part of the Church rejects the authority of the

An Unborn Catholicism

State. The English Catholic, or High Churchman, asserts that his Church is a church, and
therefore subject to no authority outside itself.
But he too cannot find the authority within it.
He says that the Church of England is part of
the Catholic Church; but this the Roman
denies; and the Catholic Church of the English
Catholic has no actual existence, even for him,
since there is no actual man, or body of men,
whom he will obey. It is perhaps in process of
becoming, but it does not come.

So at present English Catholicism is an inn
rather than a home. Those who accept it are
passing on, either to Roman Catholicism or to
some greater freedom. But often they remain
in the inn, because there is no Catholic freedom
to be found. Yet, among the English Catholic
clergy, if not the laity, there is the hope and
the promise of a Catholic freedom. They do
believe utterly in Christianity and try to practise it. They try to make the Church of England the church of the poor, and often they
succeed. The charge that their Catholicism is
a silly game and make-believe is false. In their
ritual is the return of the sense of beauty; only
they have not yet made it quite their own. In
their faith is the return of Christianity; only
they cannot yet quite express it, and cling to
old formulæ so that they may not lose hold of
it. They think themselves conservatives; but

they will not find their true faith until they become revolutionaries in thought, as they often are in politics. If they can do that, still keeping the Christian tradition, they will conquer England, so far as it can be conquered by faith.

As for the Modernists—they too are not Catholic yet. But it is unfair to criticize them as a whole, because they are not a whole. They consist merely of a number of individuals, often able and sincere, who are thinking about religion individually. The Modernist Churchman wishes to remain in the Church, not for the sake of his salary, but because he loves the Church and believes in it. He no more wishes to leave it than a man wishes to deny his mother if he is forced to criticize her. This affection of the Modernist—an affection almost natural—is not understood by those who cry that he ought to leave the Church. To him the Church is still a most important part of religion. He is a member of it, as he is an English citizen ; and he thinks that he has a right still to live within it and to attempt to work those changes upon it which he desires. He is not bound to leave it because he does not believe every article of its creeds. He knows, as a matter of fact, that no one does believe them all literally ; and no authority has laid down exactly which of them must be believed and which may be taken not to mean what they say, or to mean nothing at all. He is no more a traitor than an Englishman is a traitor to his country if he wishes England to be a republic yet still takes off his hat when " God save the King " is played.

But the weakness of the Modernists is this—that most of them are critical rather than creative ; and they are apt to harbour theories merely critical and produced by the destructive criticism of a past generation. They have not seen that the defect of modern Christianity, whether Roman or English Catholic, is that it has not enough dogma. They still cling to the notion that Christianity must be made acceptable by ridding itself of dogma. But if Christianity is to prevail now, it must do so, not by expressing a number of good intentions so vaguely that anyone can agree to them. It must convince us that the universe is of a certain nature, and that we have to live according to that nature. The Roman or the English Catholic now can be considered orthodox and yet hold utterly unchristian beliefs about the nature of the universe and of man. For instance, an English Roman Catholic peer lately wrote to *The Times* to say that, since man was a fighting animal, it was absurd to dream of a league of nations. Yet, because he believes in the Virgin Birth and the infallibility of the

Pope, he is held to be orthodox. His Church does not tell him that man is not a fighting animal, and that it is the duty of men, as Christians, to believe in a league of nations and to work for it. That is why I say that the churches have not enough dogmas, while many of the dogmas they cling to are irrelevant, since they do not prevent those who hold them from believing faithless nonsense about the nature of the universe and of man.

The Modernist has not seen this; he has been content to attack the doctrine of the Virgin Birth negatively, as being merely historically untrue—not as being philosophically or religiously untrue, or at least irrelevant. He has not a Christian faith of his own, more passionate and more precise, to offer instead of the part obsolete and altogether too vague faith of the churches. So he too fails to overcome the world, in spite of his learning, his sincerity, and his patience.

In England to-day all churches and sects fail to convince because not one of them can achieve a harmony between the rich and the poor, the ignorant and the educated, a harmony both of belief and of action. The Roman Church, as I have said, is often the church of the poor, and of those prosperous and educated people who have some weakness for which they seek a cure. But it is not the church of the great mass of the naturally religious, both rich and poor, because of its insistence on authority, and also because it offers no political hopes to the world. It tells men, or inclines them, to be content with the *status quo*, whatever it may be. Having always its own politics, it is not interested in the politics of mankind. They are, to it, secular; but Christianity will not be itself until it insists that no politics are secular, that the political aim of mankind is to establish Christ's Kingdom of Heaven here and now on earth, and in all human institutions. This it can do only by insisting that the universe and man are of a certain nature, which it must define and express both with precision and with passion. Early Christianity prevailed because it brought an immense hope into the world; Christianity can prevail now only if it renews that hope in the terms of our own time and in relation to our problems. At present no church and no sect does that.

There is the Salvation Army; but it is possible only for the poor. It is evangelical in the old sense, offering men individual salvation. It can, and does, cure them of drink, but there is no philosophy in it, no political hope. It talks of the Blood of Jesus, but not of the nature of the universe. Its one aim is immediate rescue—a noble aim, no doubt, but altogether hand-to-mouth. It is concerned with what it shall do to comfort an overworked charwoman ; it has no faith by which it can change the world so that charwomen shall not be overworked.

No one can doubt the achievements of Christian Science. It has a right to the word science, in that, unlike all the churches, even the Roman Catholic, it does teach a science, a technique, of life, and one that actually works. It says, " Live thus and thus, not merely so that you may go to heaven, but so that you may live well here and now, judged by any actual standard." It has, in fact, some understanding of Christ's doctrine of the Kingdom of Heaven ; but, for it, the Kingdom seems to be altogether within us. It would, of course, deny this ; but in practice it does seem to be guilty of the heresy of mere immanence without transcendence. The Christian Scientist believes, like the follower of the New Thought, in the Christ in himself ; and he tries to educate, to draw out, that Christ—a task for which he needs much leisure and pains. That is the weak point of his faith. I cannot imagine Michelangelo, or Beethoven, or Christ himself, as a Christian Scientist. They were too much absorbed in the Kingdom of Heaven outside themselves to be always thinking of it within themselves. Christian Science does provide a cure, but it is a self-cure. The great passionate lovers of the world, the great Catholics, might have lived more seemly lives if they had tried to cure themselves ; but they would never have done what they did do. The Christian Scientists save, and do not spend themselves ; their aim is to make beautiful works of art of themselves ; but the great lovers make works of art of something else.

Perhaps Christian Science was born in too prosperous a society ; anyhow it seems too prosperous and too satisfied a religion to prevail in England now. It is a kind of Salvation Army for the well-to-do who suffer from nerves. I would not sneer at them or at the faith that cures them ; but it is not and cannot be Catholic until it aims at working a change, not only on the inner minds of individuals, but on the whole order of society.

III

" Seek ye first the Kingdom of Heaven and its righteousness ; and all other things shall be added unto you." That saying is the essence of Catholic religion, the religion never yet realized. Also, " Blessed are the pure in heart for they shall see God." But these new faiths of technique are concerned, not so much with the Kingdom of Heaven, as with the very best of the things that shall be added. I read lately a tract, not of Christian Science, but of one of the New Thought sects. It began, well enough, by saying that we must try to find the Christ in ourselves. But then, suddenly, it let the cat, that is the self, out of the bag. If you find the Christ in yourself, it said, you can achieve whatever you wish to achieve—health, power, wealth. Trust the Christ in yourself, and you can do all things. It is one side of the doctrine of Christ, but only what he said in his passionate, exultant, humorous way. By faith you can move mountains ; but the important thing is, not to move the mountains, but to have the faith ; and if you try to have the faith so that you may move the mountains, you will not have it. You may hypnotize yourself, but you will not see the Kingdom of Heaven. You may be a success, but you will not be a Catholic. Besides, the people who do succeed thus are not attractive to others. We may wish for their success, but we do not wish to be like them. A Catholic faith would draw us through our desire to be like those who hold it.

As for the Theosophists : their doctrine of the transmigration of souls, and of Karma, has this defect, that it is devised to explain things, and to justify the ways of God to man. Things are what they are—the very iniquities of the world are what they are—because we are paying, or being paid, for the past. The Theo-

An Unborn Catholicism

sophists profess to make their faith out of the best in all religions, to have reached, by an eclectic process, the permanent religion of mankind. But nothing could be more contrary to the most profound and surprising part of Christ's teaching than this doctrine of Karma. According to the doctrine of Karma, the essence of God is justice; he has devised a universe in which everything has to be paid for, in which the past rules the present, causation controlling spirit as it controls matter. But, according to Christ, God transcends justice, and spirit can free itself, can become part of the utter freedom of the Kingdom of Heaven. God is not a judge, nor has He made a fixed, rigid, systematic universe. He has given to man a creative power, by which he can free himself of the past and rise into the eternal life of the present. Christ did not preach a doctrine of Karma; he said, "Thy sins be forgiven thee. Cease to trouble about them. Sin no more; be a new man." And he told men to make a new world by forgiveness, which is forgetting the past in each other. He told them to judge not, so that they might be like God, who does not judge. But these sayings of his have not been taken seriously, because men have not seen the philosophy in them, the profound, difficult view of the nature of the universe and of life which they imply.

III

More Essays on Religion

The effort of the Theosophists to find justice in the universe, as we see it, is based upon the conception of a static universe, with its future all involved in its past. In that conception there is no hope for the wicked, the weakling, the degenerate. As they have been, so they will be ; the best they can do is to consent to their evil fate because it is the result of their own past. But Christ says there is not justice in the universe, because its future is not involved in its past, because it is free and growing, because all life, in so far as it is life, shares in the spontaneity of God. Faith is seeing reality, not with the eyes or always, but at heaven-sent moments which rule the life of faith. And, in this reality seen by faith, there is no payment or punishment or law imposed from outside, but an infinite possibility for all men, because, having life, they have their share in the spontaneity of God. They are not what they have been, but what they are trying to become. The grace of God, if we will to accept it, is supreme and omnipotent in us ; and it comes to us, not as a reward for past virtue, but because we will to accept it now. Above all, we must not consent to the iniquities of this life as being part of the divine order. There is no divine order, in the old materialist sense of causation and law. What is divine is the creative power, which can give to man a new nature and a new world to live in—the power that is within him if he will see it without him.

Compared with this faith, theosophy, like the old scientific determinism, is retrograde. Indeed, it does express the old scientific determinism in a religious form. It is a kind of Calvinism orientalized. But the religious effort of our time is to escape utterly from all kinds of determinism, to see the nature of man imaginatively, in terms of spirit, in terms of our highest values. And we are beginning to be aware that Christianity has maintained that effort for nearly two thousand years, with many failures and perversities, but not utterly in vain. In the nineteenth century the great advance in scientific knowledge seemed to cut the present mind of man off from its past. It was assumed that, before that knowledge came, men could not think rightly about anything. Religion, and even art, belonged to the childhood of the human mind ; philosophy was a vain effort to discover what could not be discovered : but now men were at last discovering what could be discovered ; they saw a new earth, and no heaven, and were immensely complacent over their own disillusionment.

Well, the war has cured us of that complacency. The new earth is but the old one, the mind of man is as blind, as bloody, as super-

stitious, as ever. The Germans, whom we all
hailed as the leaders of the new age, have
reverted to a pre-Christian mythology. Their
God is a tribal Jahveh, and they are the chosen
people, though they assert it in a new scientific
jargon.

There are some who say that Christianity
has failed, as if it were likely to succeed when
men did not believe in it. Certainly it has
failed to make men believe in it; and that
failure is absolute, if we hold that Christianity
is something revealed once for all two thousand
years ago. But to hold that, is to misunderstand Christ himself. He professed to be a
visionary, that is to say, one who saw the
truth, as other men see a cow in a field; and
his aim was to make men see this truth. He
could not reveal it in a series of statements, any
more than one could reveal a cow to those who
had not seen it. All that he said was an effort
to make men see it, to give them his own
vision. So we can now try to attain to his
vision, undiscouraged by the failures of the
past. For these very failures, implying as they
do efforts constantly renewed, prove that for
two thousand years men have not been able
to escape from the belief that Christ had a
vision, that his Kingdom of Heaven was a fact
which he really beheld with his inner sight,
and that we can behold it also.

An Unborn Catholicism

In England, now, faith means more and more faith in the Kingdom of Heaven, as a fact which can be seen, as an order to which man, by his own effort and the Grace of God, can belong. The words " The Kingdom of Heaven " are constantly used by the religious as containing some meaning which has to be discovered. There is a great impatience with the churches because they have not discovered, or even tried much to discover, what those words mean. Their old dogmas say nothing about the Kingdom of Heaven, and therefore seem to be irrelevant. They are for the most part concerned with some state of being not our own ; but Christ says that the Kingdom of Heaven can be seen, and we ourselves can become part of it here and now. In that doctrine is the missing element of Christianity, the reason why it has failed always to be itself. The Christian Scientists supply part of that doctrine ; they tell us that the Kingdom of Heaven is within us ; but the whole of it has not yet been grasped by them or by any church. The question remains, which no one yet can answer, whether any existing church has the energy to grasp it, to free itself from its own past, to proclaim the truth that Christianity is yet to be discovered by all the powers of man's mind, and to be practised by all the energy of his will. If not, we may dare to predict that a new Church will arise and destroy the old ones. But, in England, it certainly has not arisen yet.

IX

The Pursuit of Happiness ∽ ∽

I

WHEN I gave a lecture with this title
to the Fabian Society in London,
during the most miserable period of
the war, my very chairman began by protest-
ing that happiness must not be pursued.
There we were, all of us unhappy together in
the midst of a great unhappy city, with
another great unhappy city hating us and
plotting against us oversea—both cities doing
their duty as bitterly as they could and pre-
ferring it to happiness, as men have always
done for thousands of years; and still my
chairman must needs protest against the
temptation of my title. If I or anyone else,
he thought, could once persuade men to pursue
happiness, they would be following the shadow
and losing the substance for ever.

That is what the divines and moralists have
been telling us for centuries. Even the
painters—at least the bad ones—have sup-
ported them : they have painted their alle-

gorical pictures of mankind vainly pursuing happiness in the form of a winged elf or will-o'-the-wisp; and men have looked at these pictures, however ill painted, and said, " How true ! "

But were all these warnings needed ? Were not the divines and moralists and painters preaching to the converted ? If I read history, if I observe other men or myself to-day, it does not seem to me that we are in much danger of pursuing happiness, or that we have profited much in body or soul by our refusal to pursue it.

The Germans, for instance, refused firmly to pursue happiness when they seemed to have a good chance of attaining it. Mr. Owen Wister, in his *Pentecost of Calamity*, tells us how their orderly well-being before the war made him wish to be a German rather than an Englishman or a Frenchman or even an American. They seemed to have learned a secret unknown to the rest of us, a secret from their own orchestras, the best in the world; they did all things with momentum and purpose and power—and we know what use at last they chose to make of their power. If they had used it in the pursuit of happiness, would they have done worse by themselves or the rest of mankind ? They have suffered so much that now there can be no word or feeling

The Pursuit of Happiness

for them but pity. And we in England, who seemed to have the world at our feet after Waterloo—should we have done worse if we had pursued happiness instead of riches? Should we have been less rich than we are? It may be that, if we pursued happiness, we should miss it ; it is certain that, in pursuing riches, we made poverty, just as the Germans, in pursuing power, have put themselves at the mercy of their enemies.

But let us leave the present and the immediate past and consider the evidence of religion all through the ages. In all the diversity of religions many must be false ; they must express the instincts rather than the reason of mankind. If men had ever been in danger of pursuing happiness, they would have made happy false religions for themselves and would have rejected them only when they proved disastrous. If you must tell yourself lies about the nature of the universe, why not tell yourself pleasant lies? Why not believe that there is a God who likes mankind as they are and will reward them for being what they are? Why not believe that we shall all go to heaven when we die? But no religion that I know of has ever affirmed anything so pleasant as that.

There was the paganism of the ancient world, which many suppose to have been gay and careless. But Lucretius, like any modern agnostic, found, or tried to find, freedom in not believing it. He said that, if there were gods, they cared nothing about mankind ; and this indifference seemed to him better for mankind than the caprices commonly attributed to the gods. The Greeks and Romans did not believe that their gods were good-natured, or that, when they died, they would all go to the Elysian Fields. And, as for the Jews, their God was a jealous God. He hated all other nations and did not care much for his own chosen people ; at least, He was constantly angry with them and made them angry with each other. Their whole religion, except that of a few great visionaries, commanded them to refuse happiness and to make themselves, and, still more, foreign nations, as unhappy as possible.

You may say that in all these religions mankind have expressed their experience of this life ; but, if they had ever pursued happiness, they would have devised a religion to express something happier than this life. They would have said, unconsciously, " Let us believe that which will make us happy." Their very will to power, according to Nietzsche's theory of it, would have impelled them to assert about the unknown future what would have given them joy, vitality, in the present.

The Pursuit of Happiness

If the pursuit of happiness were instinctive in man, like the instinct of self-preservation, that pursuit would express itself in cheerful affirmations about the nature of the universe; and, since no primitive religion has ever made such affirmations, we need not fear the instinctive pursuit of happiness as a danger to the morality or the reason of mankind.

The instinct of self-preservation itself certainly does not impel men to the pursuit of happiness; the more they are subject to it, the more they are filled with fears rather than hopes. It was that instinct which made men and women sacrifice their first-born to Moloch; which made the German, like the lobster, encase himself in shining armour; which set the English toiling desperately against each other and refusing pity to the poor, because they said the nature of the universe was such that it made pity a dangerous, misleading passion. No doubt it seemed so to the fathers and mothers who sacrificed their children to Moloch. They would have pitied and spared if they had dared; but Moloch, that is, the nature of the Universe, was against pity, against happiness. And who told them that, except themselves? We do not believe that Moloch revealed it to them; but still our divines tell us that God forbids us to pursue happiness; and, if we no longer believe in a

God, still we think that nature forbids us. The refusal of happiness, the fear of it, is deeper than any difference of creed. If there is no God to be malignant, there is still the nature of things, still the struggle for life imposed on us for ever, so that we are still ready *propter vitam vivendi perdere causas.*

And yet, nearly two thousand years ago, there was a happy affirmation made about the nature of the universe, and in one of the sacred books of the Christian religion. " God is Love," said St. John the Divine, or some other visionary—the name does not matter. There could not be a happier affirmation than that ; yet it was spoiled by the statement that whom God loveth He chasteneth. If Christendom had really believed the words of St. John, it would never have believed those other words ; for the love which chastens because it is love is not really love to us at all. We know the kind of parent who is always chastening his children because he loves them so well ; the children resent the chastening all the more because of the reason that is given for it. " It hurts me more than it hurts you." The very saying is a byword to us now ; but still we impute to God a state of mind which we ourselves, as parents, are outgrowing ; still, though we may say that God is love, we cannot believe that the love

The Pursuit of Happiness

of God is of the same nature as the love of man.

Yet one who has greater authority even than St. John with Christians tells us that the love of God is of the same nature as the love of man. He has gone out of his way to assert that whom God loveth He doth not chasten. He has indeed made affirmations about God, and so about the nature of the universe, so daring, so contrary to what anyone had ever said before, that to this day we ignore them.

The Parable of the Prodigal Son is constantly read in our churches, but it is not listened to. If it were, Christians would be forced either to believe it or to reject it as spurious. They escape from the difficulty by not knowing what it says. No doubt the words of that parable are familiar to everyone who reads this ; but I would ask the reader, for once, to take the sense of them seriously. Remember that Christ clearly implies the behaviour of the father in the parable to be the behaviour of God ; and now consider what that behaviour is. Note, first of all, that the Prodigal Son repents only when he has spent all his money and can get nothing to eat but husks meant for the swine. " When he came to himself, he said, How many hired servants of my father have bread enough and to spare, and I perish with hunger." That is the reason he gives to himself why he should go home. It might be the text for a satire on human nature and on the reasons why men repent. But Christ does not use it so.

And now turn to the father. He loves his son but he does not therefore chasten him. On the contrary, " When he was yet a great way off," he " had compassion, and ran, and fell on his neck, and kissed him." Then the son made his speech about having sinned; but still there was no chastening in reply, no improving of the occasion. The father—who, remember, is God—seems to have no sense of responsibility at all; he is foolishly, frivolously, pathetically happy, just because this poor creature has been driven home by his empty belly. He calls for the best robe and the fatted calf. He says, Let us eat, and be merry. Merry! He shocks the grave elder son with music and dancing. And note this also, that, when the elder son is angry and will not come in, this father, this God, does not put him in his place. He does not say, Remember, please, that I am your father. He " came out and intreated him." The elder son talks sense and justice, speaks of his years of service and obedience—yet he had never been given a kid. But even this sense and justice do not anger the father; he replies, still without any spirit, " Son, thou art ever with me, and all that I have is thine. It was meet that we should make merry and be glad; for this thy brother was dead and is alive again; and was lost and is found."

But is it not the most beautiful story in the world, and the most daring? If we could see that father behaving so, we should weep happy tears; and if we could really believe that his behaviour was the behaviour of God, how foolish would all our worldly wisdom and most of our religion seem to us! But do we believe it, even if we profess and call ourselves Christians? I lectured on this parable once at Oxford, and in the discussion which followed, a clergyman reminded me that we were not told what happened the next day. Then, no doubt, the father recovered from his first joy, and said and did all that we should expect of him. That clergyman, perhaps a little crudely, expressed our common refusal to believe what Christ affirmed in the parable about the nature of God and the universe. Christ said that God is really good, according to our deepest and most instinctive idea of goodness; that He is what we at our best would wish Him to be; but we cannot nerve ourselves to believe that the innermost desire of our hearts is true; we are afraid of the God within ourselves, whom Christ and all the great visionaries would declare to us.

More Essays on Religion

They say that this God will tell us how to be happy if only we will listen to Him ; but we will not listen because each one of us thinks that the God is only in himself, not in other men, and still less in the universe. There is a conspiracy against this God within us, so that, if we obeyed Him, He would lead us into danger. Therefore we must always deny ourselves, and Him, and follow the devil, whom we call duty, common sense, patriotism —a hundred names with which we conceal from ourselves the fact that he is the enemy of man and man's happiness, an enemy that man imagines and clothes with power against himself.

We talk of the seven deadly sins ; but there is one behind them all that we cherish and never speak of : the one deadly sin whose name is fear, the sin that we clothe with power against ourselves and incessantly disguise as a virtue. For fear, being always ashamed of itself, is always becoming unconscious. It escapes from its own pain by becoming hatred ; hatred indeed is the barren negative emotion of fear trying to be positive ; it is fear taking the offensive and becoming proud of itself as if it were courage. And fear can pretend also to be religion and philosophy. When the

The Pursuit of Happiness

great visionaries try to deliver us from it, it says that they are dreamers or blasphemers. So the scribes said that Christ cast out devils by the help of the devil; and he replied that, to believe thus the devil of fear, when it pretends to be wisdom or holiness, is the sin against the Holy Spirit, the God within us.

In our long struggle with circumstance we have inherited a fear of the essential malice of circumstance, as something which will surely frustrate us if we aim at that which we most deeply and permanently desire; and so deep is our fear that we will not confess, even to ourselves, what we do most desire. There are times when the words of a great visionary or the music of a great artist force us to confess it for a moment. The Parable of the Prodigal Son, the reconciliation of Lear and Cordelia, which is the parable of the Prodigal Father, the divine compassion of Mozart—in these we recognize what we desire for ourselves and for all men. Then we see that happiness and goodness kiss and are one; but, in a moment, we say, " This is art, or the Bible; this is a beauty, a happiness, denied to us by common sense, by each other, by the very nature of things. I myself may long for it, but I am alone in my longing, and I must suppress it lest men should think me a fool. I must run away from the very thought of this happiness, to business." It is beauty still to us, but it is not truth; the truth is that we must still fight and punish and deny ourselves and each other the happiness whispered to us by the God within us.

But Christ dared to say that this beauty is truth. In his parable he was an artist; but he went further and said, " Act according to this art, for it is the very nature of God." How little has Christianity understood him in its faint insistence upon forgiveness as if it were a painful duty. In his parable Christ presents it, not as a duty, but as a pleasure; and many of us, if we met the father of the parable in real life, would condemn him as a hedonist. We should say that he forgave his son, not for his son's good, but because he enjoyed forgiving him. But, according to Christ, to enjoy forgiving is the attribute of God, and so the highest virtue in man. There is no final opposition between duty and happiness, or even pleasure. Perfect love casteth out fear, even the fear of happiness; and Christ seems to prefer the word happiness to the word goodness; he does not say, Good are the meek, the merciful, the pure in heart; he says that all these are blessed, which means happy.

The beatitudes seem negative, to many Christians even, because they do not understand that all the renunciations implied in them are possible only to those who are allured by the positive happiness that Christ promises. Still, we believe that man does naturally pursue happiness and that, if he is to be saved, he must renounce it and pursue goodness. But man does not naturally pursue either goodness or happiness, not so much because he is foolish or evil, as because he is not yet himself at all and has no clear or single aim in life. We are not born knowing what we want; we are not born with any singleness of self or of desire; and the true aim of life is to attain to that singleness. When we speak of humanity as something existing already, we flatter ourselves; the very word is but a prophecy for us, meaning what we shall be when we have become ourselves and know our aim.

But the word also warns us that we cannot become ourselves by ourselves. The individual does not exist, and can exist only by attaining to a right relation with other individuals. Humanity is not an abstract thing, something which exists already apart from men; any more than beauty is an abstract thing which exists apart from beautiful things. Humanity is, or will be, men in a right relation with each other, as beauty is things in a right relation with each other; but the relation that makes humanity is one altogether right; and how are we to find the test or proof of this rightness ? That is the question men have always answered wrongly ; they have not dared to say that happiness is the test, the symptom, of this rightness. Often they have blindly pursued happiness for themselves alone, and have done so—as it seemed to them—against their own consciences, not knowing that they could not pursue happiness for themselves alone, any more than they could play lawn tennis by themselves alone ; the lonely pursuit of it proves that they do not know what it is. And, finding that they could not pursue it alone and get it, they have despaired of it altogether, and have told themselves that it is not to be pursued. Denying it to themselves, they have denied it to others also ; they have never seen that they can get it for themselves only by giving it to others.

Here I seem to be talking platitudes. Every preacher says that we can be happy only by making others happy ; but those who say that so glibly do not convince either themselves or others of its truth, for they never state it rightly. It is not that we can achieve happiness only by denying ourselves for the sake of others ; rather it is that happiness, in its nature, is a common thing, a right relation between us all which we have to achieve ; and until we achieve it, we cannot deny ourselves

The Pursuit of Happiness

or sacrifice ourselves, for we have not yet achieved a self to deny.

When Keats said that this world is not a vale of tears but a vale of soul-making, he meant that it is a vale of self-making. The error latent in all our opposition of egotism and altruism is the assumption that already we are selves to be indulged or sacrificed. The egotist is really one who tries to indulge a self he has not yet achieved ; and the altruist often is one who tries to sacrifice a self he has not yet achieved. If they both knew that their task was to attain to a self, and that it can be attained to only by a right relation with other selves, they would cease to argue with each other. It is the delusion of an achieved self that makes men hard with each other, and also with themselves. It gives them the wrong sense of sin, the sense that they and others are born ready-made and wrongly made ; that they are tied and bound by their own past, and must punish each other and themselves for it.

This sense of sin is merely intimidating and cruel ; it makes us look back to the past, whether of ourselves or of others, and think of all things in terms of the past. We and others have to pay for the past, and it is our duty to exact payment ; we are debt-collectors for God. We cannot forgive, because, what a man has been and done, that he is for evermore. But the true Christian doctrine insists that we can escape utterly from our past, because we are merely raw materials, all of us ; our task is not to mortify an evil self, in ourselves or others—a self that does not exist—but to achieve a self, which, again, we can achieve only by entering into a right relation with each other. And according to this doctrine there is still sin and a just sense of sin ; for sin is the refusal to enter into this right relation, to attain to the self, and the freedom of the self, which is offered to all men by the very nature of the universe ; and the right sense of sin is the sense of refusal, and of the great thing refused. This sense is not intimidating or cruel ; it does not make men judge and punish and condemn each other or despair of themselves. It makes them aware, not of a law broken, but of a heaven renounced, and, more than that, of a great gift offered and coarsely rejected. For, even if we do not believe in God and His desire to draw us all to Him ; if we cannot see Him as the father in the parable ; still, we are all blindly and pathetically offering happiness to each other and at the same time refusing it when offered.

All mankind is, if only we could see and know each other, like a family that loves each other but quarrels incessantly over the breakfast-table, and talks always of its quarrels, not of its love. A family exists and lives together for the sake of that which we call domestic felicity; and in unhappy families what secret repentings and yearnings there are! How often those who cannot meet without bitterness pity each other! all together they are missing a common happiness; willingly would they forgive each other for all bitter things said, but they cannot forbear saying them.

And so it is with all mankind. The Christian doctrine that we should love each other is not merely a command laid upon us by a God utterly and unintelligibly superior to us all: it is also the counsel of our own hearts, and that is why we know that it is divine. It is not a task imposed on us against our own natures, but the whisper and prophecy of our very selves that are not yet achieved, the promise of the happiness that we might win. If that were not so, Christianity would never have been even the ideal that it is; and those who insist that it is a revelation from without do it a poor service. It is also a revelation from within; it is what we ourselves hope, when we are not despairing. That is why hope is one of the three " theological " virtues; men who hope logically and consistently about their own nature and the nature of the universe must be Christians in faith; and they will lose their hope and their faith, if they are not also Christians in conduct, in love.

We fail still to be Christians in hope and in faith because after so many centuries we have not achieved any technique of conduct. Christ tried to teach us one in those of his sayings which seem to us most paradoxical; in them he pointed the way to happiness. But those sayings are too exalted and passionate for us; and we cannot reconcile them with the prose and routine of our lives, as we must do if we are to live according to them. What we need now is to translate them into prose, for we cannot go through life always at the height of emotion, always loving and forgiving and pitying; we need a technique that we can take as a matter of course, without strain or the sense that we are doing something surprising. The professional Christian, who is always turning the other cheek, is surprised by his own goodness; he is mirthless and uneasy, therefore not really delightful to us; he is a parvenu saint, who never makes us wish to be like him. He has the aim of self-denial, but not the aim of happiness. A right technique would aim at happiness, not as something romantic and far away, to be achieved only in another world by irrational acts of self-sacrifice in this, but as a state properly

The Pursuit of Happiness

normal, to be achieved by rational conduct here and now.

When we are told to love one another, to love our enemies, it seems to us an impossibility because we think of love as a state of rapture—men fall in love—and who could now be in a state of rapture with the Germans ? So love seems to us a passion fit for heaven rather than for earth, where we continue prosaically to dislike each other. But as we like ourselves, so it is possible for us to like each other ; as we tolerate ourselves, why should we not tolerate each other? And what we need is a philosophy, a logic, of toleration ; out of that alone can love arise. The man who is most at ease with himself is he who knows himself to be an absurd creature, the mere raw material of a self, and who is always good-humoured with himself even in his worst failures, because he expects them. So with the same good-humour we may be at ease with each other ; and out of this good-humour, this sense of human inadequacy as something absurd yet delightful, because full of infinite promise, love will spring.

A modern version might be written of the Parable of the Prodigal Son, without its intense and surprising beauty, but so that it would seem natural and probable, with the father a humorist, a good-humorist, forgiving his son easily, because he can forgive himself and is therefore constrained by the logic of forgiveness. And, if we fill out the original parable for ourselves with our own imaginations, we shall see that there must have been fun in that music and dancing and feasting; it was not all a ceremony like a service in church. The father laughed, and then the prodigal laughed; everyone laughed and was merry, except the elder brother, who was thinking about the kid that had never been given to him.

But " in our light, bitter world of wrong " we are always thinking about the kid that has not been given to us, except a few divine humorists; we forget our own absurdity in the thought of each other's sins; we put away happiness so that we may make an example of each other. Above all, we do not believe that any man will ever confess that he has sinned unless we pull long faces at him —the very thing which makes him deny his sin, even to himself. Now we insist that the Germans must make some national confession of their sin, if we are to forgive them. Many of us have looked forward to that confession as the final proof of our victory. But, so long as we all preach at the Germans, they will never confess; so long as we say they are a people unique in wickedness, they will repeat to themselves that they are unique in virtue and oppressed by the envy of mankind. That is human nature—a fact to be acknowledged in all technique of conduct. The way to make a man repent is to forgive him before he repents, as we ourselves would wish to be forgiven : and to forgive him, not as a surprising act of virtue, but in good-humour, because we are all absurd and all need forgiveness. If we all had our deserts, who would escape whipping ? Needless to say, we must prevent men from doing wrong, if we can ; but in the spirit of policemen, not of avenging angels ; for we are not angels, and vengeance is not ours.

Life is hard for us all and full of snares and temptations. One man fails in one way, another in another ; but we all fail, and we have no right to say that another man's, or another nation's, failure is worse than our own. We have no right to put any man or nation outside the pale ; we are not gods, with the right or power of damnation, but men, with the common promise of a humanity to which none of us yet has attained, or can attain without the help of all.

If we would attain to happiness and to a Christian technique, we must govern our behaviour to each other by the axiom that no man is to be judged by his past ; that we can help each other to freedom, to life in the present, to the creative power latent in ourselves, by forgiving always, not with ceremony, as if we were doing something unnaturally good, but as a matter of course and with a smile, as a mother forgives her child ; as the father forgave the son in the parable ; as people forgive each other in the operas of Mozart. They are comic operas because all the people in them are absurd, like mankind ; but they are comedy that surpasses tragedy in its beauty, because their laughter ends in forgiveness, being the laughter of men, not at, but with, each other.

And is not that laughter a thousand times more serious and profound than our fits of righteous indignation, when we forget our own sins for thinking of the sins of others ? Those fits are frivolous because any theory of the universe reduces them to absurdity. If there is no meaning in the universe, why are we angry ? But if it has meaning, then we are all children of our Father which is in heaven ; and which of us is not absurdly inadequate to that lineage ?

But always it is said, we must not encourage the evil-doer ; we must make an example of him. We have been making an example of him for ages, but with little success ; and, even if it were good for him, it is not good for us. " Spare the rod and spoil the child."

The Pursuit of Happiness

Mr. Dooley, I think, added the comment that, if you don't spare the rod, you spoil the parent. We might now try to be a little less self-sacrificing in this matter of punishment, might think of ourselves and our own characters more than of the characters of the criminals whom we labour so vainly to reform. We have built up a society on fear and punishment, and then we wonder that we are as far from happiness as ever; or we have told ourselves that happiness can never be ours, that we ought not even to aim at it. But is not that blasphemy, the only true blasphemy, as being a denial of the goodness of God? Is it not possible that, if we really and consistently aimed at happiness, we might discover what it is and so at last achieve it?

X

The Problem of Martha ∽   ∽

I

AN American lady has asked me to discuss a problem which, since she is troubled by it, must exist for you in America as for us in England—the problem of the many women for whom, as she says, " Life is going by like time spent in a trolley station, waiting for a car that is indefinitely late and whose destination is unknown." Such women, she adds, do not rebel; "they are only mildly cynical, for they do not consider it well-bred or intelligent to go bawling about the stale, flat unprofitableness of all the life they get a chance at."

How are they to be cured of their *malaise* and indifference ? or, rather, how are they to cure themselves ? for no one else can cure them. This lady is not to be put off with vague talk about finding an aim in life. " It takes more intelligence and will," she says, " to mark out an arbitrary course and follow it, where one has no guiding inclination and taste, than most men of the highest genius evince."

I would not, myself, put it that way, but I see what she means. Men of genius never mark out an arbitrary course : they are at one in conscience and inclination. With the whole of themselves they wish to do what they do ; and they excel in doing it because there is no friction within them. I do not think that will or intelligence is ever employed to mark out an arbitrary course and to follow it : a course that is arbitrary is one imposed, by whatever means, from outside, and the function of will and intelligence is to discover and pursue the course sought within. All doctors now know that it is vain to tell listless patients to " take an interest in something." Their disease itself is that they cannot take an interest in anything, and they are not helped by the advice to go and cure themselves. There is some conflict within them which, unknown to themselves, prevents them from taking an interest ; and they must be shown how to end this conflict.

Of course, most of the women of whom this lady speaks are not invalids ; but there is a conflict within them which leaves them no overflow of energy ; a little thing may turn them into invalids, and often does. They live from hand to mouth, without momentum or reserve of power, occupied with trivial tasks which they perform without knowing why. Life to them is like a meal at a bad, pretentious restaurant, where all dishes taste alike and never of themselves; how are they to get the taste of things in themselves?

It is vain to preach at them, for what right has anyone to preach? and they may return the compliment. They may tell us busy, eager people that we are busy and eager because we have not the wit to see what shadows we pursue. The worst of preaching is that it begets preachers; anyone can do it to others, but the only useful sermons are those we address to ourselves. Yet we may say to these women—a thing they know too well already —that what they need is a faith; and we may help them to it, not by suggesting some faith ready-made and to them arbitrary, but by reminding them of the rudimentary faith which they, in common with all human beings, possess to start with: the faith which itself makes them discontented with their life as it is. This faith, at first hearing, is not satisfying, for it amounts only to this—that there is latent within them a further faith which they might discover and believe; and that, if they have not discovered it, the reason is in themselves—not, perhaps, in any sin of theirs, but in some inner, unconscious conflict which can be ended if it is known. This rudimentary faith, lacking, I believe, in no one, will give hope, as soon as it is clearly stated, since it will give a preliminary aim in life, namely, to discover the conflict and by discovering end it.

We are learning more and more certainly that it is useless to set your teeth and say you will do or believe this or that, so long as the conflict within you remains unperceived. Your first task, the task set you by your rudimentary faith, is to discover the conflict, and then, one way or another, to end it. There is a mental sanitation needed, so that your will and conscience alike may not be slowly poisoned. If you are a Christian, you will not believe that God sets you impossible tasks ; if you are not, you will not believe that "Nature," or anything else, sets them for you ; the very sense of impossibility or futility is itself a sickness that can be diagnosed and cured. To believe this, is the rudimentary faith that promises a further faith on which you can act and by which you can live—one that will grow within you and be utterly your own, and yet universal.

Now the commonest of hidden conflicts in women is one between the just desires of the spirit and some duty imposed and performed but resented. So long as it is hidden, it cannot be ended ; often, when it is discovered, the victim can end it at once. The desires of her spirit become to her her duty, and she achieves that unity of the self which always she has unconsciously desired. Often this conflict is between the desires of the spirit and particular, imposed duties ; as where an unmarried daughter " sacrifices herself " to exacting parents, and all the while dislikes them for the sacrifice they exact of her. She is set a particular problem, and no one can advise a particular solution without knowing all the circumstances.

But the conflict from which many women suffer is, I believe, more general. It is between the desires of the spirit and a general vague sense of duty or obligation. This sense, indefinite, threatening, and exacting, both irks and constrains them ; there are always things they must do, yet they get no satisfaction from doing them because they do not see why they should be done. What they really wish to do with the whole self never presents itself clearly to them. All life is to them provisional, " like times pent in a trolley station, waiting for a car that is indefinitely late," because of this obligation imposed on them from outside ; and by whom or what ?

It is, I believe, imposed upon them by their own fears, of which they are unaware. If you

The Problem of Martha

told them that their lives were ordered by fear,
they might deny it angrily ; they might prove
to you that all their conscious actions are
brave enough. But often those who suffer
from unconscious fear do conceal the fact
from themselves by acts of conscious bravery.
Fear, being entirely negative and so entirely
unpleasant, always seeks to disguise itself in
some positive transformation. In the conscious mind it becomes anger, or hatred, or
even a desperate kind of courage. But these
disguises do not remove the original fear ;
the only way to do that is to be aware of it.
The way to happiness is by confession of our
deepest cowardice ; that is the true conviction
of sin, without which we cannot be saved.
It is not conscience, but the unconscious, that
makes cowards of us all ; for the fear we face
we can deal with.

But the commonest disguise of hidden fear,
in modern educated men and women, is
cynicism ; the lady who has suggested this
problem to me says that the women she has
in mind are mildly cynical ; they would not
consider it well-bred or intelligent to be violent.
In this cynicism, with its facile, impotent wit,
the thwarted spirit makes a safe and so futile
rebellion. No one minds the cynic ; she may
laugh at the machine, but it works just the
same ; her omelettes are made without the

breaking of any eggs. It is only in words that she has her revenge; and she is allowed it so long as she does not proceed to deeds. Cynicism, in fact, is the art of those who dare not be artists, the courage of those who will not confess their own cowardice. If we knew this, we should none of us be cynics: we should look for the fear of which our cynicism is a symptom; should seek joy in faith and not in the denial of it.

But this mild cynicism, so common and so enervating to the mind that enjoys it—what fear does it disguise? Usually, I think, the very fear that it repudiates: fear of what "everybody" thinks and does and says. There is something, commonly called the "herd instinct," which makes us do, say, and even think things because other people do, say, and think them. I do not like this name for it, because it implies that it is an inheritance from our remote animal past, which may not be true. It may rather be a result of our long efforts to civilize ourselves, to become social beings; it may be a kind of superfluous momentum, an irrational habit attached to an effort in itself entirely rational. The phrase "herd instinct" is dangerous because it seems to imply that we cannot overcome it. Often those who talk of the herd instinct tell us that our morality, our values, our whole mental content, are products of it. In which case we may name it and dislike it, but we cannot resist it ; for it is ourselves.

Those, however, who are aware of their instinct to do things merely because other people do them, can resist it. They can face the fear of the world, if once they confess it in themselves. They can distinguish between what part of convention is rational and what irrational, what part eases and what irks them. Only, they must, first of all, be aware of their own fear of convention, they must confess it to themselves, and observe its workings in their own minds. To rail against convention in others will not help you to resist it in yourself. The world is full of men, and especially of women, who rail and obey, who are unconventional in small things and conventional in great. It is full of cynics, the iconoclasts of toy idols, who worship the great tyrannous idols without even knowing it.

II

Women, I believe, are at the same time more subject to convention than men and secretly more rebellious against it. It imposes on them incessant duties or obligations which they perform without satisfaction or inward consent. And, the more they perform them, the more these obligations increase ; so that life seems to them to be all duty without any pleasure, and the mind all conscience without the unity of conscience obeyed. They are disciplined like recruits drilled by a stupid sergeant; it is always "eyes right" and "present arms"—exercises imposed because they are against the grain. The recruit must be broken in, must lose his self in the army or herd; and all the while the drill-sergeant who gives these tyrannous commands is an abstraction, and the victory to be won far away and in an unknown cause.

There are all these trivial, meaningless duties to society; but how society will profit by them, or what, ultimately, society is after, remains unknown. Only the recruit obeys, lest something dreadful should happen to him if he disobeys. This something dreadful is general disapproval, and it imposes an alien, unvalued conscience on those who fear it. They are for ever doing things they do not wish to do, without asking themselves why they should do them; why they should spend so much time in tidying the house, to satisfy, not their own æsthetic standard of neatness, but an exterior one; or why they should wear clothes that cost so much time and money yet do not express their own sense of beauty. Neatness, smartness, in home and in dress, is the only ideal; and it is an ideal abstract, general, and imposed. The real self in every woman wishes to be neat, not as an end but as a means ; wishes to be individual, expressive in clothes and furniture ; and often it dares not, without even knowing that it dares not. It is this secret fear that imposes the tyranny on others : because I am afraid, I am resolved to make others afraid. If I could confess my own fear, I should wish to free others from it also.

And then there is conversation—rightly, the means of communication between spirit and spirit, but often, in fact, the repeating of what everybody says and nobody means : often, too, a combination of the present against the absent. Fear makes you wish to form a party, to take the offensive, to criticize lest you be criticized. It is the opposite of the Christian truth—Judge not that ye be not judged. For the more we judge each other, the more others judge us, their fear of our judgment taking the offensive. Even intellectual conversation is often like the food in a bad, pretentious hotel, or like fashions in clothes. There is assumed to be, somewhere, a great intellectual process carried on by writers and professors, of which the noise is heard in books and magazines ; and this noise is echoed in conversation. But the real intellectual process is individual ; it must be your own, or you have no part in it : it must come out of your own experience, if it is to have precision, conviction, beauty, or joy.

America and England call themselves free ; but they will never be free in fact until we all, and especially women, have learned to rebel against this imaginary intellectual process, which is not ours or anyone's ; until the phrase, " think for yourself," ceases to be a formula and becomes a fact. We cannot acquire opinions by buying a magazine, or even a book. There is no need for us to have opinions that are not our own, earned by knowledge and experience. Democracy is merely a tyranny so long as it is the rule of a majority which does not really exist, and against which every individual unconsciously rebels ; a majority which is merely a composite photograph, unlike every individual, expressing only the abstract irrelevant part of every one, as our pictures of Christ express centuries of misunderstanding. I believe, as I have said, that women submit more even than men to this tyranny and yet secretly rebel more against it. Certainly it imposes on them petty, meaningless, and joyless duties, more than on men ; and they have naturally more sense of duty, a sense which is abused by the duties imposed on them. Civilization presents itself to them as something huge, complicated,

The Problem of Martha

and threatening ; demanding far more than it gives, yet seeming to be a reality without any alternative. Thus unconscious rebellion increases within them like a cumulative poison, and robs them more and more of hope, energy, gusto. As Blake says, " He who desires but acts not breeds pestilence " ; and where there are many desiring but not acting, unaware even of their desires, there will be a malaria of the mind, cynicism, and that absence of love which is apt to express itself positively as dislike, if not as hatred.

It is a fact, I think, that women look at each other more coldly, critically, even hostilely, than men do ; they expect to be judged, and they judge so as to be beforehand. But the standard by which they judge is often not their own ; and upon trivial points, they cannot give reasons for it and would resent being asked for them. Nothing is so intimidating, nothing lessens initiative, joy, happiness, faith, so much as the sense that you are being judged on points which you can neither foresee nor understand. It makes you feel like a new boy at a bad school, afraid of some irresistible, irrational tradition, to be revered without reason, which has grown up without you and yet is your master. The boy cannot know it, and yet is punished for not knowing it ; so he will do as little as possible until he knows it ;

and, when he does, he uses his knowledge to impose the same tyranny on other new boys and to punish them for their ignorance.

I would not speak thus freely of women's fears, if I did not believe they were greatly the fault of men. Men laugh at them, but are not aware of their own sins, so often the secret cause. For, deep down in all the conventionality of women, even of women the most consciously unconventional, is sexual fear, the fear of being thought disreputable, and, still more, of being treated by men as if they were. The social tyranny of women over women, I believe, has its origin in this fear. They are all in a union, not only to preserve their sexual rights against men, but also to make it clear to men that they are members of the union ; and it is an unwritten, almost unconscious, rule of the union, that they shall not lay themselves open to any misunderstanding. A man shall be able to know a member of the union at a glance, by her behaviour. It is not temptation that frightens a member of the union, but the thought that she might lose her status, without committing any sexual crime, by a mere breach of the rules ; the fear that women might think she was not respectable, and that men might behave to her as if she were not. This imposes a certain behaviour, a certain dress, a certain kind of conversation even. They must all be, like Cæsar's wife, above suspicion.

I may be told that in America, unlike our profligate Europe, this is not so. I do not know that we are more profligate than you are; but Englishmen tell me that you have better public manners than we have. You still retain the remembrance of a scarcity of women, which produces respect for them, since, where women are scarce, they are all wives or potential wives; and you have no tradition of a superior class which may behave as it chooses to the women of an inferior class.

All this I can well believe; but still I doubt whether you can have freed yourselves from the ancient fear of sexual misinterpretation. For there are, I take it, sexual irregularities in America as elsewhere; and wherever they exist, wherever there are profligate men, women are members of a union against them, with union rules and taboos and fears, often unnecessary and tyrannous.

At any rate, I would suggest this sexual fear as an explanation of social tyranny; and the greater the indignation aroused by my suggestion, the more I shall be inclined to believe it true. American women pride themselves upon being free, and yet there is somewhere in their own minds an obstacle to complete freedom, an obstacle that robs them of faith, aim, joy, conviction. May it not be, lurking deep in their passionately pure minds, the fear of being thought disreputable—an utterly groundless, unconscious fear, and for that very reason the more difficult to detect and expel ? I put the question, and an answer in merely patriotic terms will be no answer. I speak, not as an Englishman, but as a human being to other human beings ; and all human beings are more deeply alike than different.

It has often been noticed that women who conspicuously defy convention on one point, especially if it be a sexual point, are most conventional on others. George Eliot, for instance, just because she lived with a man not her husband, was ruthless to her own Hetty Sorrel ; she could not think freely about the passions ; she was afraid lest the world should think she herself had sinned through passion. Priding herself upon her freedom of thought, she was not free ; and the fear she would not confess to herself made her as sensitive to criticism as a wound in the flesh is sensitive to the touch. There was a wound in her mind that could not be healed, because she would not confess the fear that kept it raw. And, because she was afraid of the world, she saw the universe as ruthless to sin and forced herself to believe that ruthlessness just. Perfect love casteth out fear ; but the converse is true, that fear casts out love; and George Eliot, in her novels, is a judge, rather than a lover, of women.

But Charlotte Brontë writes with freedom; she is not afraid of the world, like a boy who has never been to school, like a young home creature, full of loves and hatreds, but all of them free—her own and unimposed. Yet a woman writing of *Jane Eyre* in the *Quarterly Review* said that, if the author were a woman, she must be one who had forfeited all claim to respect from her own sex. There was the union feeling : the resentment against one who laid herself open to misinterpretation ; the desire to break her in, to teach her the rules ; and the envy of her unbroken spirit, which could express itself in terms of beauty and passion without asking, " What will the world think of me ? "

III

Now a diagnosis of all mental trouble is half-way to a cure. But it must be a diagnosis which convinces the patient, and one which he himself can carry further. Know that you fear, and what you fear, and your fear will begin to weaken. For, when it is known, you rebel against it with all your will ; you act against it, and so prove it less terrible than it seemed. But when fear is unconscious, and so known only by its effects, which, being cut off from their cause, seem a necessary part of your own nature, then these effects are indeed terrible to you. To see the connexion between the fear and its effects is to see also the remedy. A plain task is set to the will, and it is braced to the accomplishment of that task.

At this point faith comes in, that rudimentary faith of which I have spoken and which I can now state more precisely. It is the faith that further faith will come by knowing your own weaknesses. Learn to know and forgive yourself, and you will learn to know and forgive others. Then you will no longer be afraid of them. This great intimidating world of everybody will consist for you merely of other women, afraid like yourself of the great intimidating world that does not exist. They will amuse you instead of frightening you, just as you will amuse yourself. For if once you can see that you, being a human being, are forgivable and lovable, however ridiculous, you will see that that is true of others also. But, because we never will confess that we ourselves are ridiculous, we cannot forgive ourselves, or others.

In the war, contrary to all expectation, a greater courage than ever before was shown on both sides, in spite of the fact that few soldiers had ever seen a shot fired in anger;

and the greatest courage was shown by the most civilized armies. The reason, I believe, was that, in the most civilized armies, certain rudiments of psychology had been learned. In the past it was believed that, to conquer fear, you must never confess it to yourself. That is believed still by all savage peoples, with the result that they are brave enough until a sudden panic breaks out among them. after which they are but a terrified mob.

But civilized man has learned to say to himself, and to his fellows, " I am afraid ; I am a coward by nature ; we are all cowards by nature ; we should all like to run away." The fact of fear is no longer a guilty secret which each must conceal within himself : it is common knowledge, an enemy that all have to face. So the soldier, confessing his fear and facing it from the first, is far less liable to sudden panic, especially when confronted with some new devilry, than ever before. Further, since he faces his fear and even talks about it, he suffers less often from sudden nervous collapse. It is the man who " has never known fear " whom sudden panic, sudden nervous collapse, overtakes. The savage, or the man who does not know himself, is not so good a soldier as the man who does know himself ; and so it is in all the trials of life. Life is not entirely a matter of moral problems ; we cannot do everything with the blind will, or, rather, it is part of the moral problem to know yourself, to manage your own will, to confess your weaknesses so that you may overcome them. The Christian doctrine of conviction of sin, rightly understood, is good psychology as well as good morals. Be aware of your sin and it will no longer be terrible or devilish to you ; it will be merely human, and you will see how to overcome it, and with it the fear which is your sin.

So I would suggest to women whose life is aimless that, before seeking an aim, they should ask themselves honestly whether they are not afraid of " everybody," and whether this fear does not impose upon them a number of duties which are not real duties to them. Let them say to themselves, like the modern soldier, " I am a coward and I know it." Let them say this also to each other, so that the consciousness of a common cowardice may grow among them ; for the fear of everybody is a common enemy, a common disease, which may best be fought by all in common. People catch it from each other just because it is concealed ; and they may also catch the antidote to it, if it is not concealed.

Fear, powerful as it is, has this weakness, that no one really wishes to feel it ; we cling to our fears and side with them because, trying to escape from them the wrong way, we turn them into something more positive— hatred, judgment, self-approval. But, once convince anyone that these feelings are but disguised fear, and he will try to rid himself of them so that he may be rid of the fear. Thus women, now that we begin to understand something about our own minds, might make a collective attack on their own fears by means of a collective confession of them. They might begin to criticize the social obligations which seem to be imposed on them in the light of this new self-knowledge. " Do we do this," they might ask, " because we really wish to do it, or because we are afraid of each other ? " There is, of course, a common belief that the sense of duty is necessarily based on fear ; that, if fear is abolished, the sense of duty will go with it ; but this belief is itself a result of fear, a fear of human nature and, indeed, of the whole nature of the universe.

IV

There is another conception of duty, based, not on fear, but on hope, namely, that it is identical with the desire of the whole self, if only that desire can be discovered. When we have a desire that seems to us contrary to our duty, it means that there is a conflict within us ; it means either that our sense of duty is not a sense of the whole self, or that our desire is not of the whole self. According to this view, the whole self as a unity does not exist, to begin with, as something either good or bad ; it is something to be achieved gradually and by continual effort ; and, when achieved it will be good. As Keats said, this life is not a vale of tears but a vale of soul-making, by which he meant a vale of self-making. When the self is made, then duty and desire are identical ; and we know from our own experience that happiness, power, faith, mean the identity of duty and desire. It may happen to us rarely, but, when it does, then we recognize it as being the very aim of life suddenly and gloriously realized. But, where the conception of duty is separated from the conception of desire, there human beings are always fighting a losing battle : either desire or duty, both a part of them, must be worsted ; and, whichever wins, the self is impoverished of a part of itself. This, then, is to be aimed at—the identity of duty and desire ; and both duties and desires are to be criticized in the light of that aim.

It is a common error of professional rebels to rail at morality, duty, convention, just as blindly as they are obeyed by the mass of men. We cannot do without duty or convention ;

indeed, the rebels are themselves conventional ; they form a small herd or crowd of their own in their very rebellion. What is needed is a clear discrimination between righteousness and convention. It is not in itself righteous to walk on one side of the path because others do so ; but it is convenient ; and it would be unrighteous to rebel against this convenience and cause inconvenience to others, merely in order to assert your own freedom from convention. But where conventions are themselves inconvenient, it is important to see that they are not duties, that it may be duty to break down their tyranny by asserting the rights of desire against them. Thus, if a woman has no time to read, to think, to practise some art for which she has a natural talent, because all day she is performing duties imposed on her by what she takes to be public opinion, then it becomes her duty to herself, and so to the world, to assert her own just and natural desires, and to gratify them, so that she may be a human being, with joy, vitality, and purpose, and not a mere automaton resenting the fact that she is one.

If we are unhappy, we make others unhappy ; if we are happy, we make others happy, not by any conscious effort to do good, but by the mere contagion of the realized self. The world now is full of people who disseminate unhappiness, discouragement, vague fear, disbelief in the rational order of the universe, by their own lack of purpose and lowered vitality. Often they seem to be energetic, but it is the energy of a machine doing something that nobody wants done; and it is an energy distressing to witness because it is always exhausting itself, threatening a nervous breakdown, communicating to others its own aimless unrest. This kind of energy we all resent with a blind, natural inhumanity, just as we should resent the presence of some one with an infectious disease; but our resentment is futile, and merely increases the disease. What we need is a diagnosis which will make us humane. The blind energy exhausting itself comes of a separation of duty and desire, comes of a secret fear lest desire should master duty; and, where this fear is, there cannot be happiness or that harmony of the self which alone produces efficiency.

It is vain to rail at such " martyrs to duty " as slaves of convention—one might as well rail at influenza patients as slaves of bacilli. What is needed in both cases is a knowledge of the disease, its cause, and cure. The cure will not work in a moment; we are only at the beginning of self-knowledge; but at last it has begun. For ages man has been gaining power over the external world, but without

The Problem of Martha

any increase in self-knowledge, and so in self-control. The task for man now is to know himself, to enter upon a new age of achievement.

And, first of all, he needs to confess that, with regard to self-knowledge, he is still in the Stone Age. All our morals, our conventions, our scientific method even, have been evolved blindly in the past of self-ignorance ; but at last we are being driven to self-knowledge by suffering. We see that it is useless to tell sufferers, including ourselves, to be men and overcome their troubles. We are not yet men, or women, because we do not yet know ourselves. But, with the desire for self-knowledge, with the first glimmering conception of what it means, an immense hope has entered the world. We see that the best of the old morality, that which appeals not merely to our sense of duty but to our hearts, is itself based upon the intuitions of genius. Pity is more understanding than judgment, for those who value pity most are those who know themselves best. Those who judge always do so because they have no self-knowledge. But, beyond these beautiful but blind affirmations of the Christian faith, we need now the knowledge that will make them, not less beautiful, but no longer blind.

" Martha, Martha, thou art careful and

troubled about many things." It is not
enough to say that with pity. Martha must
know herself why she is careful and troubled,
so that she may free herself from her troubles
and cares.

XI

On Jonahs ❦   ❦   ❦   ❦

REASON AND THE RUN OF LUCK

THERE is still a firm belief in Jonahs at
sea ; and the other day a sailor, who
was prosecuted for failing to join an
Admiralty transport, pleaded in excuse that
he was known to seamen generally as Jonah
and that the sailors in the transport had
threatened to throw him overboard if he did
join.   Certainly, if superstition ever could be
rational, they had some reason for theirs.   He
had served in the *Titanic* and the *Empress of
Ireland*, both of which were wrecked, and in
the *Lusitania* and *Florizan*, both of which were
torpedoed.

It seems a pity that sailors should know
the story of the prophet Jonah, since they get
only one moral from it. The book was certainly
not written to instruct seamen how to deal
with Jonahs.   There are several morals to be
drawn from it, some of them subtle, but that
is not one of them.   Yet it is unfortunately
the only one which sailors seem to draw.

Jonah is probably the character best known to them in the Old Testament ; and what they know about him is that he caused bad weather through his own fault and was very properly dealt with by his fellow-voyagers. They forgot, if they ever knew, that the sailors cast lots to discover who was the cause of the bad weather and that the lot fell upon Jonah : also that Jonah himself confessed to them his disobedience and told them to throw him overboard.

The Jonahs of modern times are not discovered by such means, nor do they ask to be thrown overboard. They are assumed to be Jonahs because they have been uncommonly unfortunate. Perhaps they are pitied as well as shunned for their misfortunes ; but often enough it is assumed that they have done something to deserve them, and then the superstitious fear of their fellows becomes cruel.

The worst of it is that a Jonah may himself share the superstition, and may be unnerved by the thought that he is marked out for misfortune ; he may even come to believe that he has committed some crime which marks him out, in which case he is on the way to madness. But even landsmen, who believe themselves free of superstition, are apt to be intimidated by a run of ill-luck. It unnerves them ; and the wisest of us, if unnerved, are prone to superstition. Even if we resist it we can see that superstition is a natural growth of the human mind, that superstitious explanations lie in wait for us all and are but the expression in thought of our animal fears, the invasion which those fears make upon the reason.

Hence the great value of psychological curiosity ; it enables us to explain ourselves to ourselves, to detect the irrational when it disguises itself as the rational. We are naturally myth-making creatures, and the story of the prophet Jonah is only an excuse and a pattern for myths which we instinctively make about ourselves or others. If there were no such tale in the Bible, sailors would believe in Jonahs under another name or under no name at all ; they would think that there was some reason for a run of ill-luck and that it must continue unless by some means the curse, whatever it may be, is removed. And they have, of course, countless tales to support their belief in Jonahs, tales which cannot be refuted, however false they may be.

The worst of superstitious tales is that they often are true, that men do have extraordinary runs of ill-luck in life as at cards. The superstition lies in the conclusions that are drawn from them. For in life, as in cards, a run of ill-luck is against the average, and sooner or later the average will right itself. Therefore, sailors, if they are to consider luck at all, should welcome a Jonah on board ; for the longer his run of ill-luck has been the more he may expect good luck to adjust the average. If we have tossed up heads ten times running, we expect, whatever mathematicians may say, to have a run on tails, unless, of course, there is something wrong with the coin. But, in the case of a run of ill-luck, superstition always suggests that there is something wrong. That is the devilish cunning of our animal fears ; and the only way to frustrate it is to be against superstition altogether, in small things as in great— in fact, to cultivate an almost irrational disbelief in all superstitious tales. Even if they are true, they do not mean what they are taken to mean. The belief in Jonahs is contrary to the order of the universe, as man most slowly and painfully, by the use of all his spiritual faculties, has discovered that order. Whatever the explanation of extraordinary events may be, the superstitious explanation is not true. To entertain it for a moment is to enervate the mind and to misinterpret the universe. That may not be safely done even in trifles, for none of us is far enough away from the dark fears of the savage to take risks. We need to be almost superstitious in our fear of superstition, as a reformed drunkard needs to avoid wine.

XII

The Remedy ✑ ✑ ✑ ✑

A REVIEW OF TOLSTOY'S "CHRISTIANITY AND
PATRIOTISM"

THIS book, which, as Mr. Garnett tells
us in his Introduction, is scarcely
known at all in England, was provoked
by the visit of the Russian Fleet to Toulon in
1893, and by the sudden enthusiasm over
the Franco-Russian Alliance. What disgusted
Tolstoy in that enthusiasm was the automatism
of it. All artists dislike automatism, since it
makes men alike, when, for the artist, their
interest, their beauty, their reality consist in
their differences ; but for Tolstoy, as a pacifist,
a Christian, a friend of man, this automatism
was not only ridiculous but a threat to all that
he most desired. He describes the rejoicings
in both countries, and insists that they were
irrational and artificially induced. The two
nations suddenly found that they loved each
other, but

this sudden exceptional love of the Russians for the
French, and of the French for the Russians, is a lie ;

and our implied dislike for the Germans and mistrust of them is a lie too. And it is a still greater lie that the object of all these unseemly and senseless orgies is the preservation of the peace of Europe.

His Puritanism betrays itself in his disgust of all the eating and drinking; he prints the menus of banquets and seems to think that the love of good food and drink is part of the collective insanity. There was, he tells us, a Russian sect who believed that the end of the world was coming, and who therefore began to do no work, dress in smart clothes, and eat sweet things. So the French and Russians thought the millennium was come and feasted like the people before the flood. Tolstoy himself died before the deluge came, but wrote this book fearing and expecting it. It is shrewd, eloquent, amusing; it tells the Russians, the French, and all of us many bitter but wholesome truths—truths which, even when they were written, many of us would have admitted to be true; and yet they had no effect whatever, and those who in all European countries acknowledged those truths were powerless to prevent the catastrophe.

Indeed, Tolstoy himself has no remedy, except to denounce patriotism, by which he means what we should call nationalism. He insists that once patriotism was necessary and performed a real service for mankind.

The Remedy

When the more civilized nations were surrounded by barbarians, their equals in power, patriotism meant the preservation of civilization against those barbarians, with whom no terms could be made, since their one aim was plunder, and since they could see only the temptation and not the value of that which they would destroy in enjoying it. But the civilized nations now are patriotic, not against the barbarians whom they can mow down with machine guns, but against each other, though their interests are really common as their civilization is common. So that which was once a virtue has become an obsolete and dangerous passion. This is true if by patriotism we mean nationalism, the belief that your own nation is superior to any other, and that it can preserve its power, its civilization, only by war. And it is significant that many Germans were induced to consent to the war by the belief that their civilization was threatened, as in the past by Tartars, now by Russian hordes. Their Government did, with a cunning perhaps unconscious, revive an obsolete fear and an obsolete passion ; and there remains always a danger that this fear and passion may be revived in any country, so long as the masses are subject to induced automatisms.

But, as we read this book, the question

forces itself upon us, where is a remedy to be found ? It is always easy to be aware of past automatisms, to smile at them as we read of them in his history ; we can talk calmly enough of " The red fool-fury of the Seine," but the problem is to be on our guard against fool-furies when they are our own. Mr. Garnett in his Introduction says that Tolstoy under-rated the inherent vitality of nationalism. He did indeed ; and we know now that all the common arguments against war, though we may admit their justice in the abstract, are utterly vain against a concrete case of national anger, fear, enthusiasm. There is something noble in nationalism itself, something which, as the psychologists say, needs not to be sup-pressed or destroyed but sublimated ; the pro-blem is to understand it and to sublimate it, and this cannot be done by preaching, even when Tolstoy is the preacher.

In his last chapter he speaks of a remedy. It is " that every individual man should say what he really thinks and feels, or, at least, should not say what he does not think." There speaks a Russian who, living in a country where all freedom of political thought was suppressed by the Government, believed that nothing is needed but such freedom. He was not aware that to think freely, to discover even what you really think or feel, needs more

The Remedy

than political freedom ; it needs a training of the mind that shall protect it against its own automatisms and the automatisms suggested by others. Tolstoy himself speaks of the power of propaganda ; but does not seem to be aware that it can be practised upon men politically free, so long as they are ready to believe what they wish to believe. Governments, he says, " fear the expression of independent thought more than an army ; they establish a censorship, they bribe the newspapers, they seize the control of religion in the schools ; but the spiritual force which moves the world slips away from them . . . it lies in the depths of men's consciousness." It certainly does ; it lies so deep that men themselves are not aware of it. In democracies, because they are unaware of it, they themselves establish the censorship, and fear the expression of independent thought more than an army. They have a power of ignoring the truth, and those who tell it, which is greater, because more unconscious and more unanimous, than that of any despotism.

The remedy then is not to preach against war like Tolstoy, or to argue against it like Mr. Norman Angell, but to discover the unconscious causes of it in the human mind. We have read this book with eagerness, with amusement, with sympathy, but finally with disappointment. We knew all this before the war, yet that knowledge did not prevent the war. Christianity has been preached for nearly two thousand years, and anyone can see that it is incompatible with war; but Tolstoy prophesied that "the bells will begin ringing, men with long hair will dress up in gold-embroidered sacks and begin praying murder"; and his prophecy came true, because we do not yet know ourselves, because we believe that we are rational beings by nature, when in fact we have to make ourselves rational by acquiring a knowledge and mastery of ourselves, as we have acquired it of external things. What is needed is a great and combined scientific effort to understand the collective insanities of the human mind, which are far more dangerous and common than individual insanities. Men must, by means of self-knowledge, protect themselves against the attempt to turn them into automata; they must realize that in such attempts, and in their own defencelessness against them, is the great danger to civilization and, indeed, to the human race; above all, they must realize that at present, with regard to such things, we are in a state of almost savage ignorance. Christianity itself needs far more psychology than we possess to practise it; freedom needs far more if we are to enjoy it.

The Remedy

Science, which now is almost the enemy of mankind because it provides them with the means of destroying each other, will become their friend only when they realize that they must practise it, not to make poisonous gases, but to know themselves.

XIII

Sheep without a Shepherd ✎ ✎

FAITH AND EXPRESSION

IN the matter of religion England now is in a very strange state. A few years ago it seemed to be content with its Churches and its creeds because it thought little about them. The ordinary Englishman took it for granted that they satisfied the wants of other people; and he did not inquire who those other people were. Now, suddenly, he has his own wants; he begins to ask real questions about the nature of the universe; and he has a great desire for an answer to them, not the answer given by the complacent agnostic, but at the same time one that he can believe. And he wishes it to be expressed in such a manner that he can believe it, to contain all the intellectual energy and the experience of the modern world.

Everywhere there are men and women trying to find this answer for themselves and discussing the matter with others. But they do not go to the Churches for the answer.

Sheep without a Shepherd

They are making a creative religious effort, but they have no leaders in it either clerical or lay. No one has any authority for them ; they have no tradition of theology in which they put their trust. It seems to them that religion has suddenly to be discovered from the beginning, or at least that it has to be restated altogether ; for the current religious statements, the very language of devout people, seem to them to be merely obsolete.

For instance, there are devout people who discuss the question—" Why does not God stop the war ? "—and the question itself seems to belong to a dead world. If there be a God in whom men can believe, He is one about whom such questions cannot be asked. Or a clergyman declares that the war has been sent by God to punish us for our sins, especially for not going to church. The mass of Englishmen who are longing for a faith would not attempt to argue with that clergyman. He also and his religion seem to belong to a dead past and to talk a dead language. No doubt we are punished for our sins, but not in that way ; nor, if there be a God, is He one who resents our absence from His places of worship. He has not a sense of dignity that can be wounded by us ; He does not share our egotisms. But above all, we cannot impute this or that evil to His interposition, like the lawyers who call certain disasters acts of God. The mind which does that is merely archaic or archaistic. It seems to be trifling with the great problem which is vexing the minds of men, with the great desire which possesses their hearts.

We speak plainly because the chief cause of religious indifference in the past has been the absence of plain speaking. The atheists and agnostics have spoken plainly enough, but not the people who desired a faith, who had a faith perhaps, but could not find an expression for it. They thought that the current religious expression was better than none, and tried to be content with it. But now, they are not content and they become dangerously impatient. They turn away from the churches more and more, as their interest in religion grows. And yet, more than ever, they believe in Christianity, if only they can find an expression of it that will convince their intelligence. " Blessed are they that mourn, for they shall be comforted." Those words begin to be full of meaning to thousands ; but they wish for a conception of the universe in which they may take their place, a conception in which reason and passion are at one. And meanwhile the clergy ask—" Why does not God stop the war ? "

The pity of it is that there is a Christian

theology into which all human intelligence once poured, and which might live again and convince if only human intelligence would find a new expression for it. It needs to be freed from the mere dust and litter of the past, from questions such as those we have mentioned, and from the state of mind which asks them; it needs to be taken quite seriously by those who believe in it. For they, most of all, have not taken it quite seriously, just because they have assumed that it was a finished product, accomplished and expressed once for all. But it is not and it cannot be, unless it is dead. In every age the human mind taints its beliefs with its own peculiar follies and egotisms; and if those beliefs are to live they must be continually cleansed by posterity. The time of cleansing for the Christian theology has been delayed so long that there is a danger lest the mass of men should think it all litter and dust of the past. This danger the Churches have not understood. They have believed that they could stave it off by mere adjustment and by the slow, reluctant relinquishing of this or that belief as it became impossible. What is needed is not mere adjustment or abandonment, but discovery and growth, not diplomacy and compromise, but the belief that there is a wonderful truth still to be discovered, and faith in the scent for that truth. The problem for the Church now is to open itself to the rising religious intelligence of the country, so that that may pour in and quicken it; but if that is to happen the intelligence of the Church itself must rise, and it must not be content any longer to talk pious nonsense in the hope that it will seem sense because it is pious.

The Church and Dogma

The Church must be free if it is to be alive; and it must be ready to make sacrifices for its freedom and its life. Now, no doubt, all religious people, whether clergy or laity, are ready for those sacrifices; at least no worldly motive deters them. If they are deterred, it is by fears, not for themselves, but for the Church which seems to many of them to be always fighting a losing battle against what they call " the forces of infidelity."

But these vague, ill-defined forces seem more terrible than they are. At least it is timidity, not audacity, that gives them their strength. So long as the Church seems to itself to be fighting a losing battle, so long as it is concerned only to maintain its own existence in an indifferent world, it will fight a losing battle, will fail more and more to maintain its existence, and will find the world indifferent. The mass of men are not hostile to religion; even the militant atheist of the working classes,

Sheep without a Shepherd

who is now becoming rarer, is not really hostile
to it. His chief complaint against the Church
is that it exists to maintain its own existence.
That very timidity which fears his, and all
other, attacks does actually provoke them. A
Church anxious only to preserve the truth,
as if it were some flickering light in a high
wind, seems to have no truth worth preserving.
Those who convince others that they have the
truth do so by their own eagerness to discover
it ; and it is this eagerness alone that can give
life and unity to a religious body. The fear
that truth will die, like an invalid, of any
change is itself a lack of faith in the power of
truth. Truth lives only when it grows ; it
lives on adventure and discovery ; when these
cease it also ceases to be itself.

At present there is another obstacle to every
change in the Church besides the antiquated
machinery that is complained of. It is the incessant objections which are made, within the
Church, to every detail in all proposed changes.
But what is the cause of those objections ? It
is always fear, the fear that any change will
have some evil effect upon the decrepit body of
belief. But the body of belief is decrepit and
inert because of this very fear. There is, as it
were, a hypochondria in the Church which is
itself the cause of the weakness it imagines. Its
profound irresolution is the result, not so much

of real differences within it, as of the fear lest any change should betray them. And the result is that the Church tries to maintain unity by inertia, when it is to be achieved only by action and passion. Men are at one only when they all passionately desire some high object. They are not, and cannot be, at one when they try to maintain a unity by compromise. If the Church would dare to conceive of truth as a goal, a heavenly goal to be passionately desired, it would achieve a unity in its own passion for the truth. That passion exists in many Churchmen, and it is growing among them ; but it has not yet mastered the policy of the Church itself, it has not transformed the Church from a preserver into a seeker.

Laymen often are unaware of the passion for truth that is in the minds of individual clergy ; and from a kind of prudery they fear to shock them with their own free thinking. They regard a clergyman as a shorn lamb to whom the wind of truth must always be tempered. And there is a reason for this in the extreme timidity of the Church whenever it discusses any change. It is over-tender for its own shorn lambs, whether clergy or laity. It remains as timid as its own most timid members ; it tries to be as ecclesiastical as its most ecclesiastical laymen. Before it can attain to freedom of thought or of action, it must exchange this timidity for the courage of desire. If the ecclesiastical layman chooses to be shocked by it, he must be shocked. The Church does not exist for him; or, where it does exist for him, it is no Church, but merely an antiquarian curiosity.

There cannot be freedom in any society so long as it is concerned merely to maintain itself. The effort to maintain itself will always enslave it to its own past, as the Roman Empire in its decline was enslaved. Freedom, like life, like unity, is begotten in a common passion for what is not. It is itself creative, and the result of a creative effort. Words like liberty, life, unity, are vague so long as they remain only words, so long as they do not express themselves in action. What we look for in the Church now is action, first in reform of herself; and that can only come if she is possessed by a passionate desire to achieve her own freedom, and in achieving that to achieve unity and life.

ORTHODOXY THE GREATER AND THE LESSER

There is, in the Christian faith, a greater and a lesser orthodoxy, and they may be distinguished from each other by this: that the greater is concerned mainly with the future, and the lesser with the past; that the greater makes for a future unity, whereas the lesser insists upon present difference. To the lesser orthodoxy, there is a continual insistence upon present difference, a continual effort to discover it in the smallest particulars. We need to know, for instance, the exact truth about the Communion, what does really happen in it; for unless we know that we cannot benefit by it. We have been told what the Communion does mean; and to think that it means anything else is to be disobedient—to cut ourselves off from its virtues. But to the greater orthodoxy the Communion and the whole Christian faith is something that we all have to attain to; and none of us has yet attained to it. Differences are rather a result of universal imperfection than a sign that some are right and others wrong. We cannot know what the Communion means until we have attained to it; and we can attain to it, however imperfectly, only through the desire to do so, not through the belief that we know already what it means.

It is implied in the lesser orthodoxy that there is in man no instinct for the truth; that he must be told it and believe it blindly, if he is to know it at all; otherwise his own reason will lead him wrong. And so there is no mark of the truth except in the absolute uniformity of those who have been told it and believe it. But, for the greater orthodoxy, man has an instinct, an appetite, for the truth, as for righteousness. It tells a man that he must follow this instinct ; and its faith consists in the belief that the instinct for truth and for righteousness are ultimately the same instinct, and, further, that they will ultimately, if followed, lead all men to the same belief and to the same conduct. So for it unity is always something in the future, something to be reached by men who obey the same spiritual instinct and are possessed by the same spiritual appetite. It has not yet been attained, either in conduct or in belief, because men are all imperfect, even when they are proceeding in the right direction.

Because of its faith in an ultimate unity, in the certain goal of the spiritual appetite and instinct of men, it is not much troubled by present differences. There is a truth to be discovered, a righteousness to be attained to ; but what these are we can discover more and more precisely only as we aim at them in thought and in conduct. And so men recognize this greater orthodoxy in each other, not by their present uniformity of belief, but by their common appetite. That is what draws them to each other through all present differences ; they can talk about that which they wish to attain to, and forget each other's failures of attainment, being conscious of their own. Their faith is that they will some day think and act alike, since it is a real truth and a real righteousness that they pursue ; but to the lesser orthodoxy there is always something unreal in truth and righteousness, since man has no natural appetite for them, but must be told what they are ; and one man can only recognize them in another by uniformity of belief and conduct.

To return to the particular instance of the Communion. It is in its very essence an act of public worship. Men can attain to it only together and by the admission to it of anyone who would be admitted. It would not be Communion at all if it were exclusive, if only the members of a club were admitted to it. But the essence of the Communion is, not that it is a rite imposed on men from the past, and one of which they must understand the precise meaning before they celebrate it, but that it is a common effort to attain to a certain state of being, of fellowship with each other and with God. It is rather a promise than a command, and a promise that by certain means men can attain to a certain state of being. So Communion, if attained to, does not mean something ; it is something, and men can only understand its meaning by actually experiencing it. Therefore their effort should be to experience it all together, rather than to define what exactly it means before they experience it. They should go to it as artists all working together in the production of one work of art, rather than as philosophers differing in their philosophy. And if they go to it thus they will find that there is less difference in their doctrines about it than they had thought ; for the more they attain to it the more they will see that these doctrines were efforts to state the same fact, and that they seemed so different because those who stated them had not fully experienced the fact. When the experience is one and the same, every statement of it is seen to be inadequate, and the differences are in the inadequacies. So also, in the desire for the experience, the differences will be forgotten ; Communion will be something to be attained to in the future, not something imposed on men from the past. They will be drawn together for the discovery of themselves and of God, not separated by their past theories about either.

This does not mean that we need to state the minimum of our present common beliefs and to say that that is the truth. To do that is merely to insist upon a very empty lesser orthodoxy. We need faith, not in the wisdom of any particular men, least of all of ourselves, but in the spiritual instincts and appetites of mankind. If they seek they shall find ; that

187

is what we must believe, not that we have found and that the others have lost.

Religious Union

It may be that the war will teach us at last the secret of religious harmony in diversity. Writing of " the Soldier's Chaplain " *The Times* Special Correspondent has told us that, with all the mixture of creeds, the utmost good fellowship prevails among the chaplains of the different Churches. There they are not cut off from each other by their different places of worship ; they are not rivals, but soldiers in the same cause. They perform the same offices and face death together in performing them.

We must all wish this fellowship to persist after the war is over ; and it can only persist if the experience of the war gives men a logical as well as a practical reason for it, if the different ministers of religion can find intellectual no less than emotional reasons for the friendship they now feel towards each other. Religion is the most important thing in the world, no doubt ; and that is why religious differences have been so bitter, why ministers of one creed have even thought it right to have no dealings with ministers of another. They could not be friends with the preachers of false doctrine.

But friendship itself, when they cannot escape from it, makes them see that the doctrine is not false—at least on the points of most importance. It makes them see that minor differences merely express the diversities of the human mind. One man is born a Catholic and another a Nonconformist, as men are born Platonists or Aristotelians. But the good Catholic and the good Nonconformist are both on the same side, like the good Platonist and the good Aristotelian. Both are fighting the same enemy for the same reason, and he is strong enough and evil enough to tax all their energies. It does not matter whether a man worships in a church or in a chapel, or what views he holds about infant baptism, when there is a towering unfaith about the universe and the nature of man to be withstood. The war now is, not between different theological sects, but between those who think that there is nothing worth living for but life itself and those who think that life is worth nothing unless it is lived well. Are we to be willing slaves to the struggle for life, or are we to aim at a spiritual freedom from that struggle ? That is the question, the theological question, that matters to us all; and we shall not decide it by quarrelling about matters of ritual or Church discipline. All who answer it one way are on one side, and all who answer it another are on the other, no matter what Church they belong to. There is a new division so sharp and clear that all the old divisons are obliterated by it.

That is the reason why there is so much confusion now in religious thought. Many of the old terms are emptied of content, and those who still use them seem to be talking about nothing. Often they use them in a new sense, and so are unintelligible to those who still use them in the old. Life is coming back very quickly into religion with the knowledge that there is a real unfaith, a real devilry, to be fought ; but this life is often like new wine in old bottles, for it is a new conviction struggling to express itself in old formulæ. So men find that they have the same conviction when their formulæ are different. A particular Churchman may agree with a particular Nonconformist upon essentials more than with another Churchman. It is not now the question of Apostolic Succession that interests him, but the question—What does he live for ? Is it that he may go on living, whether in this world or another ; or is it that he may live well, that he may forget himself altogether in those things which he can love for their own sake ? That is the question which is now of vital importance to all really religious men ; and the answer given to it is what puts men on the one side or on the other, whether they are Churchmen or Nonconformists, or even

Sheep without a Shepherd

Agnostics. Does worship express the love of God for His own sake or a desire to get something out of Him ? And further, is it possible for worship or any other activity of man to express anything except a more or less enlightened self-interest ? These are the real theological questions now, and the questions upon which men are divided, even when they are not conscious of the division. The whole basis of Christianity has been attacked by a new doctrine, the doctrine that man cannot really be disinterested, that he is always engaged in the struggle for life, whatever pleasant illusions he may harbour about his own nature, that he is in fact incapable of that love at which Christianity tells him to aim. According to this doctrine God Himself, if there is one, can only be loved by man for his own profit. In that doctrine the Germans have been trained and because of it they have made this war. Against it we are fighting, if we are fighting for anything that is worth the sacrifice.

So all the religious energy of the country is now united against it ; but, if it is to remain united, we must remain conscious of the real enemy and forget all trivial differences in that consciousness. We must see that these differences are merely necessary diversities of human nature and no effort must be made to remove them. The way to the unity of Christendom is not through rival proselytizing, which only emphasizes differences, but through the knowledge that they are not essential. Those who compass sea and land to make one proselyte make a hundred enemies in the process. My way may be best for me ; but it is not therefore best for others. We must assume the universal imperfection of humanity, in ourselves as well as in others, and the diversities that result from that imperfection. Such things are assumed when men face death together in the trenches ; we must assume them too when we face life together at home after the war.

COLLECTIVE SIN

Collective sin is a convenient name for those common sins which afflict a whole society with impotence, those perverse ideas which make evil seem good and frustrate all the efforts of civilization. These are, in the first place, sins of thought rather than of action. The worst of them is that the action to which they lead does not appear sinful, although it has worse consequences than actions which are obviously sinful. Being sins of thought, they are sins that come from lack of faith, from an intellectual cowardice which is itself the result of an obscure moral cowardice. Thus the whole of our society has been intimidated by the doctrine of the struggle for life—a doctrine vague in itself but producing very precise and evil effects in action. This doctrine, presented scientifically, has not seemed to be immoral although it is in direct contradiction to the Christian faith. It amounts to this—that there is nothing to be lived for but life itself, and therefore that the struggle for life is sanctified; that men will attain to the utmost possible happiness through that struggle and not through a common effort to minimize it.

There is, for instance, a common belief that the present condition of the poor is inevitable because it is the result of the struggle for life, just as the Germans believe that war is inevitable and even good in itself because it is the struggle for life organized and openly carried on. And among professing Christians there is a belief that Christianity cannot concern itself with any systematic mitigation of that struggle because it is the law of our life here on earth. Even individual interference is likely to do more harm than good; we are all subject to an iron law and in this world at least the devil will take the hindmost. Now this belief, according to Christianity, is a collective sin, and it is the reason why we tolerate so many intolerable evils. But for the belief, which acts as a narcotic upon us, we should not be able to endure these evils. Our consciences would give us no rest if we had not marked out an unmoral domain in which our consciences are not allowed to act. We say there is no remedy and therefore we relieve ourselves of the hard task of finding one; we would rather do anything than think, and we have discovered a doctrine that makes it unnecessary to think.

This state of mind expresses itself perfectly in our party system; for by means of that system we are able to dispute so incessantly about methods that we get nothing done. We think about the disputes, which is easy, rather than about the remedies, which is hard. Can we doubt that, if we had a real Christian faith and a real Christian passion to find a remedy, we should think more about the remedy than about the dispute? Because we are all honestly anxious for victory in the war our party system has ceased. We believe that we can win the victory, and therefore we combine in one party to win it. But because we do not believe that we can win a victory over the struggle for life we split up into two parties to dispute about it. Is it to be wondered at that there is a third party which disputes the sincerity of the other two?

But this ought not to be a party matter at all, and would not be but for lack of faith. There would be no question of an opposition between poor and rich if both were convinced that they could find happiness only in fellow-ship. Then there would be an end of the bitterness both of the revolutionary and of the reactionary. Now each believes in the omni-potence of the struggle for life, and therefore in his own right to be bitter against the other. Neither thinks it possible that all parties in the State should have the same purpose—namely, to improve the State and not to defend a class. Parties themselves are an expression of the inevitable struggle for life ; and one class must be the enemy of the other. This, perhaps, is not openly said, but it is acted upon ; and the Church may deplore the action, but it does not attack the underlying idea, the collective sin, which produces the action. The Church, though not pacifist in inter-national politics, is strangely pacifist in national politics. It has not its own clear notion of what a State should be, by which to judge the State as it is. It must not, it says, take part in party politics—which is true enough ; but its duty is to condemn a State in which all politics are party. Its duty is to insist very clearly what is wrong, and not to rest until there is a harmonious effort to right it ; and, above all, its duty is to attack, with a religious passion and a scientific precision, the evil ideas by which men dull their consciences to the acceptance of what is wrong. Christianity is one splendid defiance to the doctrine of the struggle for life in all its forms, new or old. It is a defiance, both moral and intellectual; and the intellect of the Church should be used, not to struggle for its own life, but to insist that men do not live so that they may struggle for life either in this world or in another. It is the duty of the Church to tell them with passionate plainness why they do live and why the Church lives.

Steps Towards Recovery

It is easy, in the criticism of actual forms of religion, to be content with mere negations, to imply that there is a true religion different from that which is criticized, but never to attempt the task of stating it. But criticism is useless without the effort to provide something better than what is criticized. There is also the danger that the critic will be misunderstood as wishing to advocate a new religion when he may be really only anxious to revive the old one. Nothing is easier than to devise new religions; it is like drawing up paper constitutions; but a religion which one man devises as an intellectual experiment is very different from a religion that will grow in the minds of men. What we need now is not a new religion, but a Christianity that will grow naturally in our minds as it grew in men's minds in the time

of the early Church, a Christianity that will
seem to be in the future as well as in the past,
that will not need to be preserved from decay
by a conscious and artificial effort.

The mass of men have certainly lost faith,
and how are they to regain it ? What is the
most essential part of faith which they can
accept to begin with, and which, if accepted
and acted upon, will grow in their minds and
lead them on to essential Christianity ? It is,
we suggest, this—that man, if he forgets himself in the love of that which is not himself,
whether it be other men or some great cause or
some noble art or science, does gain a power
from a source outside himself which is not
human at all, which is not even of nature, as we
know it. That is the Christian doctrine of love
extended and applied to all high disinterested
passion, and it is a doctrine which any man
may test for himself. But those who believe
it, even in its vaguest form, will be led on to
test it ; and, if it be true, they will be more
and more confirmed in it by their testing of it,
more and more aware of this power, and that
it comes to them from a source altogether
beyond their knowledge.

Now those who really believe in Christianity
will believe also that, by beginning with this
article of faith and by living according to it,
men will find more and more of Christianity

to be true ; they will more and more understand what it means, and what part of the old statements of it belongs to the past. What is needed is a real working faith which can be opposed to the real unfaith of our time. The real unfaith of our time is that man is utterly moulded by circumstances, moulded by his struggle for life, and that there is no escape for him from the universal pressure of this struggle. That unfaith cannot be met by mere dogmatic statements about God and what He commands us to do. It is easy enough to believe such statements and to be devout in all observances imposed by the Church and yet never to dare the adventure by which alone a man can prove to himself that he is not altogether moulded by the struggle for life. He that would save his life shall lose it. Yes, and shall lose even the sense that he really is a living creature and not a machine worked by Nature or God. The very essence of Christianity is this—that man can himself will to be free, and that he can be free in action and in thought, through love ; but that, without love, he is not free in either, but is at the mercy of the struggle for life, always struggling for it, but never attaining to it.

By love—and the meaning of the word love needs to be extended—he does become free also in thought ; that is to say, he becomes aware of the nature of reality, which is only revealed through love. And the Christian faith is that in reality he will be aware of God. But nowadays there are many who cannot start with the belief in God. The word has meant so many false things that to them now it is meaning less ; or, if it is not that, they know they cannot say truly that they believe in God. For it is a serious thing to say ; and an honest man will not say it so that he may acquire merit by doing so. But he can begin with the belief that, if he forgets himself in the love of that which is not himself, he will gain a power from a source outside himself, he will attain to that freedom which is promised by Christianity. And if Christianity is true, that faith of his will grow, will become clearer and more certain as he acts upon it. It will be the open sesame for him to the true wisdom, and by means of it he will come to see the universe not as a discouraging chaos, but as order and beauty ; and he will, perhaps, at last attain to the knowledge that there is in the universe a love answering to his love, of which he is aware only through his love.

But it is also the essence of Christianity that its faith can be a growing faith only if it is acted upon in all things. We are apt to think of Christianity now as merely concerned with morals ; but the love demanded by it of men

is far greater than a moral thing. It is all
high, disinterested passion ; and the Christian
doctrine now should be that every disinterested
passion is love that leads to the knowledge
of God ; and, further, that men must refuse
no disinterested passion, that they must not
content themselves with morals or with the
idea of pleasing God by obeying His rules.
God, no more than the sun, makes rules ; but
by love and love alone man can be led into the
sunlight of God.

XIV

The Kingdom of Heaven   ∽   ∽

I F after two thousand years Christendom
still misunderstands and even ignores
Christ's doctrine of the Kingdom of Heaven,
we might expect to find that it was not understood when he was alive. If it had been understood then, some tradition of it would have
been handed on from the apostles, the Church
itself would have existed to find the Kingdom
of Heaven, St. Paul would have preached it,
and it would not have been possible for the
very heretics to ignore it in their heresies ; all
the natural perversities of the human mind
would have been exercised on that and not on
the Incarnation. The very Manichees would
have said that the Kingdom of Heaven was not
to be seen or found in this world, and so on.

Now as a matter of fact the life of Christ, and
especially his behaviour after the entry to Jerusalem, above all at his trial, is unintelligible
and cannot be explained except on the theory
that the doctrine he preached had been misunderstood by his followers and his enemies

alike, and that he himself suddenly discovered this misunderstanding, discovered it perhaps at the moment of his triumphal entry. And what more natural ? His doctrine of the Kingdom of Heaven is peculiarly difficult to understand for this reason : it is a philosophic doctrine, but philosophers do not understand his expression of it because he does not express it in philosophic terms. But apart from his lack of a philosophic vocabulary and the lack in his hearers of any philosophic understanding, he did not express it in philosophic terms because to him it was not a theory but a fact. He with his spiritual clairvoyance saw it constantly as we all see it at heaven-sent moments. And because he saw it constantly it mastered his mind, he thought and spoke always in terms of it. It was as real to him as the material facts of life are to us. It was reality to him ; and so he spoke of it as reality, as we should speak of material facts. A philosopher used to thinking of it, if at all, as a theory would not recognize that theory in Christ's matter-of-fact presentment of it. To him Christ would be a myth-maker or a man with a delusion. He would not be capable of the imaginative feat of seeing his own theory expressed as a fact by one to whom it was a fact of actual immediate experience. For the philosopher it is at best a deduction from experience. But Christ experienced it. It is as if he saw the very courses of the stars which astronomers discover by a scientific process. What all the great philosophers have tried to establish by argument, he bears witness to from his own vision. He had, as we say, " been there." He saw with sense and spirit alike that relation of all things which is the Kingdom of Heaven, saw it as clearly as we see a cow in a field. And, if it is a reality, we might expect some one to arise with a keener sense of reality than other men and to see it and to bear witness to it not merely in argument but in his whole way of thinking, feeling and acting ; with an extreme of belief, with a certainty impossible to those who have reached their belief only by reason. It is this certainty and the manner in which it is expressed that have caused the teaching of Christ to be misunderstood by philosophers. They have not seen that he was concerned with a philosophical proposition, because he expressed it as a fact of his own immediate experience.

But if he was misunderstood by philosophers for one reason, he was misunderstood by the mass of men for another. To them the Kingdom of Heaven was a fact, but not the same fact that it was to Christ. The Jews expected a natural deliverer. Use the word Kingdom, and it meant to them something at once material and divine, for they conceived the divine in

material terms. God was he who would
deliver them from the foreign yoke. He meant
to them power, and power to be exercised
on their behalf. Kingdom to Christ did not
mean power in that sense, but rather what we
mean by the phrase—the reign of natural law.
We use the word law there as a metaphor, and
even men of science are constantly and dangerously misled by the metaphor. So, when
Christ used the word Kingdom, his hearers
would at once be misled by it. As we conceive
of all power, even that which we call the power
of nature, in legal terms, i.e. as punishing or
rewarding, so they conceived of the power and
Kingdom of God in national terms. The word
misled them from the first, and they were confirmed in their misunderstanding by the very
efforts of Christ to make them understand.

He, like all men possessed by a great truth,
insisted that he was possessed by it. Listen to
me, he said, believe me and I will show you
this truth. To the Jews that meant Listen to
me for I am your national Messiah. When
Christ said I will deliver you with my truth,
they thought he meant I will deliver you from
the Romans. The more he expressed his
spiritual certainty the more they thought he
meant a material certainty. And his own
apostles, when he said my Kingdom is not
of this world, thought he meant that he would

The Kingdom of Heaven

exercise a supernatural power and take them with him to a celestial state of power and bliss. James and John may have rid themselves of the notion that he would reign in the world as it is, that he would be a second and more successful Judas Maccabeus, but only to fall into the belief that he would accomplish a complete and celestial revolution, giving his followers a celestial status in it. That they did misunderstand him thus we have a proof in the doctrine of St. Paul. He thought at first that Christ was coming in a short time to accomplish this celestial revolution (1 Thess. iv, v). To him the saying that the day of the Lord cometh as a thief in the night means that Christ himself will descend suddenly from Heaven with a shout, with the voice of the Archangel and with the trumpet of God. "Then we which are alive and remain shall be caught up together with them in the clouds to meet the Lord in the air."

St. Paul was mistaken; and, if Christ meant that by those words, he also was mistaken. The event has proved that. But further, that meaning is inconsistent with his whole teaching and with what he says constantly about the Kingdom of Heaven. There does seem indeed to be this inconsistency in some of his actual reported sayings. Either then he himself was inconsistent or his sayings were misunderstood

and misreported. The first supposition seems
to me, and must seem to all Christians, less likely
than the last. Indeed, if Christ was guilty of
such an inconsistency his whole teaching becomes nonsense. Either he meant by the
Kingdom of Heaven what I have taken him
to mean or the mass of his most profound
teaching means nothing at all.

So, if there was misunderstanding, it is probable that the misunderstanding arose over ideas
unfamiliar to the apostles and contrary to their
preconceived ideas. We can indeed see in the
Gospels themselves signs of such misunderstanding. And where the evangelists report
sayings which they themselves evidently do not
understand it is fair to assume that those sayings are authentic. They were reported in spite
of their unintelligibility because Christ actually
said them. And if they are inconsistent with
other reported sayings, it is fair to assume that
those other sayings have been misreported—have
been perverted unconsciously to fit in with the
preconceived ideas of those who heard them.

But the doctrine of St. Paul of an immediate
second coming was in accordance with the preconceived religious ideas of the time and with
all primitive religious ideas. It is not likely
that St. Paul evolved this doctrine by himself
or that it was contrary to the beliefs of the
other apostles. If it had been, he would have

argued about it and referred to their disagreement. He does not; he assumes it as the common belief of the Church. We may therefore take it to have been the common belief shared by the other apostles; and there is much evidence that it was so shared. So on this point either the apostles were in error about the doctrine of Christ, or Christ himself had taught them what was not true. There is no way out of this difficulty. Either Christ himself based his whole teaching on a misunderstanding or an error of fact, or else his own apostles misunderstood him, did not know what he meant by his Kingdom of Heaven. It is curious that many orthodox Christians in their desire to accept the inspiration of the New Testament have preferred the former view. I confess I prefer the latter. You cannot get out of the difficulty by saying that Christ meant a second coming which has not happened yet. St. Paul and the other apostles thought he meant a second coming which was to happen in the lifetime of some of them. And if they were wrong about that they may well have been wrong about Christ's whole doctrine of the Kingdom of Heaven, about the very nature of what he meant by it. And if they were wrong, even in the matter of detail, if they believed that he said he was coming soon, that is to say, while some of them were alive, if the

apostles, living with him and listening incessantly to his words, could misunderstand him on
a point of such vital importance to them, even
though it were a point of detail, how much more
likely were the mass of men to misunderstand
him altogether.

And it is clear, I think, from the whole
gospel story that they did so misunderstand him. We find, for instance, that what
most impressed them was his miracles. The
miracle would be to them a proof that he
had supernatural power which he was going to
use for the Jewish people and against the
Romans. And the Scribes and Pharisees, while
not believing in his supernatural power, evidently thought that his aim was to overthrow
the Roman rule. They did not believe he could
do it, or many of them would have been with
him ; they thought no doubt that he would
lead some futile rising and get them all into
trouble. So they tried to trick him into some
act or word of rebellion so that they might
induce the Romans to deal with him. That is
the meaning of the incident of the Tribute
money. Further, in his trial they represent
to Pilate that he wishes to be the King of the
Jews, that is the reason why Pilate is to condemn him. The Rulers had several reasons for
killing him. Their own private reason, of
course, was not that he was against the Romans,

The Kingdom of Heaven

but that he was against them; that he preached a new religion in which they would no longer be rulers. But this new religion was not inconsistent with a national uprising. Such a rising led by Christ would, if he succeeded, make him the ruler of a victorious people and their power would be gone. So we may believe that they honestly thought he meant such a rising and that they naturally gave that design of his to Pilate as a reason why Pilate should condemn him. That was the whole point that interested Pilate. If Christ meant a rising, if he wished to be the King of the Jews, then he was a dangerous man; otherwise not.

But what the rulers believed and feared, that the mass of the people believed and hoped. In the triumphal entry they expressed their hopes. He was coming to free them at last. He would now act instead of talking. They had been submissive to his talking because a great national hero would naturally tell them of a new righteousness like all the prophets of the past. That new righteousness would be a condition of their reconciliation with God, the result of which would be a miraculous victory over the Romans. But now the talking was done with and the fact of victory was to begin. That also the rulers feared, and determined to act. They argued thus—Christ was an impostor and had not the supernatural power he claimed. So he would not be able to exercise it if they seized him. Therefore they had only to seize him to prove to all men that he had no supernatural power, that he was an impostor. Once he was in their hands, the bubble would be pricked. And that was what happened. The people turned on him with a rage as great as their former welcome. "He saved others," they cried, "himself he cannot save." Because he could not save himself he was an impostor. How otherwise explain their sudden change ? Why was his condemnation and death popular with the mob which a few hours before had given him a triumphal entry ? The bubble was pricked for them ; because they had misunderstood his whole teaching, because they had seen in him a national and supernatural deliverer which he himself never intended to be.

And the effect on Christ himself ? He himself had not known that he was utterly misunderstood. If he had known, he would have told them in the plainest terms that they misunderstood him, and this telling must have been related in the Gospels. It would have been to the apostles themselves a great, and probably dismaying, event. It would have produced on the people an immediate change and no less on the Scribes and Pharisees. They would have

The Kingdom of Heaven

seen that he was not dangerous, they could have afforded to laugh at him as a mere dreamer ; whereas as a matter of fact they were clearly afraid of him as a dangerous and very practical impostor. Christ then did not discover until after his entry into Jerusalem, or at the earliest during it, that he was misunderstood. And it is this discovery that explains his whole behaviour during his trial and perhaps after his entry. The moment he made it, he must have been overcome by an enormous despair. All his life he had been labouring to make men understand what he meant by the Kingdom of Heaven, and they thought he meant that he was a second Judas Maccabeus with greater supernatural powers. This proved that the people whom he loved and to whom he spoke were incapable of understanding a single word he said. He had concealed this fact from himself in his own certainty and eagerness for so long ; and now it was forced upon him. Every one who has ever lectured knows the feeling of despair when some one asks a question which proves that he has not understood a single word of the lecture. That was what happened to Christ about his whole teaching, his whole life.

Every one had misunderstood it—not in detail, but altogether. There was threatening a conflict about a perfectly irrelevant matter. His followers might defend him, blood might flow, his own dearest apostles might be killed— Peter and James and John—in a quarrel that had no meaning for him whatever. What was he to do except to avoid that quarrel by saying and doing nothing ? To attempt explanation was hopeless, he had been explaining for years and this illusion was the result. Therefore he said nothing and did nothing. He was ready to be led like a lamb to the slaughter, because only by his death could he hope to make men understand what he had meant. There he was like Socrates, who also died because men would not understand his life. He was accused of corrupting the youth ; Christ of wishing to be the King of the Jews. Both charges were so absurd that they could not be refuted by reason. They might be refuted to posterity by a last supreme protest of self-sacrifice. And so we find that Christ could give no explanation of himself—except to a Roman, who at least had not been listening to him and who was not possessed with this hopeless preconception.

Wearily and yet triumphantly he speaks to Pilate. My Kingdom is not of this world. I came into the world to declare the truth. He that is of the truth heareth my voice. Those who wish for the truth can understand me, others cannot. There is no more to be said. Between these two men—so different, but both

more civilized than the Jew mob, both capable
of understanding a general proposition—there
is a kind of understanding, a kind of chivalry.
Pilate treats Christ as with respect, speaks to
him as man to man, not merely as an official to
a prisoner ; and Christ responds, enough at least
to give some short weary explanation of himself. He does not say that he is a messiah,
that he has supernatural powers. He argues
as a man of sense to another man of sense. If
my kingdom were of this world, then would my
servants fight that I should not be delivered
to the Jews ; but no, my kingdom is not from
hence. He does not say to Pilate that he has
angels who would fight for him if he would,
and surely he would say this if he believed it.
He says merely that, because his kingdom is not
of this world, there is no fighting. He is the
teller of truth which he was born to tell. And
no one has understood it ; therefore there was
nothing to do but to die.[1]

[1] This conversation with Pilate is so inconsistent
with many other things in St. John's Gospel, and indeed
so far above the rest of that gospel in subtlety and
dramatic power, that we cannot believe it invented consciously or unconsciously by the author of that gospel.
It reads like the most authentic event in that gospel,
unless it was invented by one of the greatest dramatists
in the world. If so, who was he and how did it get into
a gospel written by one who was a great mystic but not
a great dramatist ? While, if it is the result of inspiration, why is it inconsistent with much else in that gospel ?

Christ then died in silence, except for some cries of agony of mind or body ; died misunderstood by all ; and has been misunderstood for the most part ever since. If we assume this misunderstanding even on the part of his apostles, we understand better why they all fled, why even Peter denied him. To them also he was, if not an impostor, at least unintelligible in all his actions. We know that he was so unintelligible to them. They could not understand his refusal to resist. They too expected him to be rescued by swarms of angels. In Tintoretto's picture those angels swarm round them all unseen at the last supper. Christ himself had spoken of them, meaning no doubt that he was safe in his own reality whatever happened to him. He was still aware of that, and could die aware of it, like Socrates ; and because of his intensity of spiritual perception, more than Socrates himself. But, when no angels appeared, the apostles would be filled with doubt and bewilderment. Peter was not merely a coward ; he came to see the end of his master, but he could not understand it. His very courage was enfeebled by his bewilderment. And at the moment of his denial, his master looked at him ; the personal power of Christ overcame him. Christ was to him simply himself, and what did he do ? He did not acknowledge him for lord, for the supernatural power he had believed him to be. He believed that no longer. But still he loved him, and so went out and wept bitterly. Christ was to him now, not a God, but a man like himself and doomed. Still he did not understand what Christ really was and meant; but he wept the tears of his heart.

So Christ was the lamb of God in a higher sense than that of orthodoxy. He died for the Kingdom of Heaven because not otherwise than by this last act of supreme disinterestedness could he hope to make any men understand what was the disinterestedness of the Kingdom of Heaven. And dimly men have understood. He has, because of that sacrifice and his manner of bearing it, been the most beloved man in history. And his doctrine of the Kingdom of Heaven has survived and still has a marvellous power over the minds even of those who do not understand it. He is not to us a great philosopher, but one who actually saw a reality and lived as he saw. But when shall we try to understand the reality he saw? When will Christendom learn the true doctrine of the atonement, the meaning of the words " that one man must die for the people " ? The Church itself has perpetuated the misunderstanding in its very dogmas. For two thousand years it has justified the despair of Christ.